OUT
of Autism

THE DAVIS AUTISM APPROACH
TOWARD FULL PARTICIPATION IN LIFE

CATHY DODGE SMITH Ed. D.

In Collaboration with Ronald D. Davis
With Contributions from Desmond Smith

 FriesenPress

Suite 300 - 990 Fort St
Victoria, BC, V8V 3K2
Canada

www.friesenpress.com

ISBN
978-1-5255-1695-5 (Hardcover)
978-1-5255-1696-2 (Paperback)
978-1-5255-1697-9 (eBook)

1.Education, Educational Psychology

Distributed to the trade by The Ingram Book Company

For Desmond, my best teacher

With gratitude to two most important Rons

Ron Davis is a humble genius who shared his understanding and vision by creating the Davis programs, particularly the Davis Autism Approach Program. Those of us who are fortunate to be Davis Autism Approach Facilitators/Coaches thank him daily for empowering us to do this joyful work: assisting those with autism spectrum disorder who wish to participate more fully in life, and who allow us to accompany them on their journeys. I have been blessed to be there from the earliest days of this program and to see the power it brings to the lives of those with ASD in my son and grandson. Thank you, Ron, for your life and work, for allowing me to be part of it, and for allowing me to create this book to share your genius with others.

Ron Dodge is my husband and my love. He is also my dearest friend, loudest cheerleader, and staunchest supporter. He never complains about how much I work, or how much I love my work. His editing pen has contributed greatly to this book. Thank you, Ron, for sharing all parts of my life. It wouldn't be nearly as much fun without you.

Acknowledgements

First thanks go to Ronald D. Davis for allowing me to write this book about his program, and to participate in this awesome work. Next is Ron Dodge, my wonderful husband, who has read this manuscript many, many times and made it better through his suggestions each time. Thanks also to Lorna Timms, Director of Davis Autism International, and Abigail Marshall, Webmaster for Davis Dyslexia Association International, for reading and making suggestions. My sister, Nancy Birchard, also read and contributed thoughtful feedback, as did Liz Webster. Jonathan Alderson, author of *Challenging the Myths of Autism*, took the time to read it and made most useful suggestions. Thanks to Liam Kelly and Desmond Smith who made all the clay models pictured within. Thanks to Mary, mother of Liam, and Cathy, mother of Matthew for sharing their stories, and to Meryle, vocal artist, who shared her Davis journey through her own words. My son, Desmond Smith, contributed his own experiences as an adult with ASD. He is also a gifted Davis Dyslexia Program facilitator and Davis Autism Approach Facilitator/Coach, and I am most fortunate to have him work with me. We are all in this together.

I am most grateful to all the professionals at FriesenPress who have helped shepherd this book to publication. In particular, Zoe McLean, my publishing specialist, was unfailingly patient, positive, encouraging and helpful.

All names of clients have been changed to protect their privacy. Exceptions to this are Liam, Matthew, and Meryle.

I appreciate all the help I have received more than I can say, but state categorically that any errors are mine alone.

Foreword

By Lorna Timms
Director, Davis Autism International

In my role as an advocate for those who seek help in addressing the challenges accompanying autism, I am constantly asked, "What can I do?" I have many varied answers depending on the needs and circumstances of the individual; however, there is now one thing that I will be recommending to all who seek my assistance—"Read this book!"

Dr. Cathy has laid out in these pages the answers most people are seeking—simple, practical, effective action. *Out of Autism* takes you on a journey of understanding as it describes the missing pieces needed to help those on the autism spectrum. It describes a set of simple techniques, which can be meaningfully integrated into daily life with ease, providing the foundation for those with autism to navigate and succeed in the neurotypical world without losing their genuine self.

I have known Dr. Cathy for many years and found her to be an incredibly genuine, highly talented, caring professional. In addition to Dr. Cathy's academic credentials, the 53 years she has spent helping people in her role as an educator, counsellor, and facilitator, equip her with the expertise to write this book. However, she also understands autism from a much deeper level—that of personal experience. Her understanding, empathy, and genuine respect for the individual comes from a deep-rooted experience of having been on a mother's and grandmother's journey with children on the autism spectrum.

As you read *Out of Autism*, you will begin to piece together how the Davis Autism Approach works—how it builds solid bridges, allowing individuals to navigate the next part of their developmental journey, the steps that their neurotypical peers take with relative ease but which have eluded many of those on the autism spectrum. Dr. Cathy has included an essential component in this book: the words of those who know, who have had the experience of this approach, and have integrated it into their daily lives. This, along with her own experience and light-hearted manner, makes it a book you will not want to put down until the last page has been turned.

I will close with a quote from a mother whose 17-year-old son completed the program:

The program just makes sense. It does not convey the message that you need to change who you are. Instead, its message is: *I get who you are. These are the tools that are going to help you become even more who you want to be ...*

Lorna Timms
Director, Davis Autism International
Mother and advocate for those who need a voice.

TABLE OF CONTENTS

OUT
of Autism

CATHY DODGE SMITH Ed. D.

In Collaboration with Ronald D. Davis
With Contributions from Desmond Smith

Out of Autism — Introduction

From eight-year-old Edwin, who thought a new electrical socket made a perfect birthday gift, to 10-year-old Dillan obsessed with steamboats, to 26-year-old Aidan, who knows every train schedule in the province, I invite you to accompany me on a journey into and out of the world of autism. This will be a four-stage journey mirroring the four parts of the Davis Autism Approach Program created by Ronald D. Davis.

Anyone who is interested in Autism Spectrum Disorder (ASD), and particularly in finding a new approach to the treatment of autism, will find this book interesting and refreshing. You might be the parents of a child already identified as having autism or being on the autism spectrum. You might be the parents of a child who has not been diagnosed with any specific condition, but who remains a puzzle to you and those who work with him[1]. You might be the parent or physician of an individual who has displayed some of the symptoms of autism—enough to make you wonder—but without access to solid information that would allow a diagnosis of autism. Teachers and therapists also may find much of interest here to stimulate the heart and mind.

You will discover in these pages a new way of understanding

---

1 One of he or she, him or her, and his or her will be used throughout this text for third person singular to avoid use of he/she, him/her, or his/her.

autism. More importantly, you will learn about an approach to treatment that goes to the heart of autism and helps a person with autism participate fully in life.

Finally, you will learn how we do it … how Davis Autism Approach facilitators/coaches can assist your loved one on this amazing journey toward becoming a "real boy." You may recognize that term from the story of Pinocchio. Ronald D. Davis was severely autistic until the age of 12. Once he began to develop out of autism, his main goal in life was to become a real person, much as Pinocchio wanted to become a 'real boy.' By that he meant he wanted to be like others and to feel accepted by others. He wanted to participate fully in life.

There is another connection. When Ron Davis was first helping people with dyslexia learn to read, using the methods that later became the Davis Dyslexia Correction program, he was called to work with a 12-year-old girl. He discovered later that she was on the autism spectrum and had never spoken, but as he worked with her, she spoke with him quite normally and learned to read. Later, she became fascinated with the Jiminy Cricket character from *Pinocchio*, and said to Ron, "I don't have a conscience." That led Ron to ask himself, "How do you create a conscience?"

It has been a long journey. In your hands, you hold Ron Davis' answers. The Davis Autism Approach helps individuals with autism spectrum disorder become 'real persons,' just as Ron Davis did—persons who have a conscience, and persons who can participate more fully in life. We invite you to join us on this journey.

PART ONE
A Little Background

In this book, you will be learning about the Davis approach to treating Autism Spectrum Disorder (ASD): the Davis Autism Approach Program. About the program, Abigail Marshall says, "It is geared to addressing a specific problem (or set of problems) rather than a diagnosis. For purposes of the program, autism might be described as *the failure to develop behaviour to the extent that the person can form and sustain social relationships*" (Marshall 2012).

Thus, it is possible that an individual diagnosed with ASD might function comfortably enough that she would not feel the need for treatment. Likewise, it is possible that an individual who has no diagnosis of autism in any of its forms would experience sufficient difficulties in social relationships that treatment would be appropriate and desired. The appropriate question to ask and answer is whether the treatment helps the individual meet his goals for participating fully in life.

Autism has had many names over the years, with all former labels currently being integrated into the one term of *autism spectrum disorder*. Those interested in learning more about the specifics of diagnostic criteria and changes in nomenclature are referred to Part Five. The summary of the information therein is that ASD can be described as a core triad of impairments in social skills, impairments in communication skills, and limited or repetitive interests and behaviours.

That entire section was originally the first part of this book, but wiser heads prevailed and convinced me to jump right into the meat of the material, and let those who wish to delve into the academic background of autism do so. However, there is one research-based issue I wish to raise here.

Of particular significance to this author is research which found that up to 95% of people with ASD can be shown to have Unusual Sensory Experiences (USEs) (Tomchek 2007). Others have found similar evidence (Ben-Sasson, Hen and Engel-Yeger 2009) (Leekham 2007). USE refers to an adverse reaction to sensory stimulation that would be tolerated easily by most people. I mention this here because I think this should be more heavily weighted in the diagnosis of autism than it is currently and may provide one explanation for the social skills challenges of people with ASD. Adults with ASD have reported avoiding social situations because the USEs they experience or anticipate make it too uncomfortable for them. I suspect that the methods used in the Davis program which gradually allow sensory experiences to be processed accurately could be one reason why the Davis program works so well. We will return to this theme later.

This work is placed in the context of the spiralling incidence of ASD, and it provides an innovative approach to understanding and treatment, bringing help and hope to individuals with ASD and their families.

PART TWO
The Davis Theory: A Different Understanding

As they worked for years with individuals who had learning disabilities, dyslexia, and ADHD, Ronald D. Davis and other Davis Dyslexia Program facilitators were confronted with clients whose problems could not be resolved with the Davis Dyslexia Correction or Davis Attention Mastery programs; some of them were individuals who were on the autism spectrum. With his own background as a child with ASD, his formidable intellect, and his engineer's mind, Ron Davis worked to develop a way to address these unmet needs.

He determined that autism was likely a functional problem rather than a structural one. He therefore saw it as a developmental disorder, one in which the normal developmental path followed by most humans did not take place, or was limited. As he reflected on his own journey out of autism, he determined that there should be a way to assist others to make that same journey. He reached the conclusion that "autism is manifested when, for whatever reason, an individual fails to complete the early childhood developmental steps of *individuation, identity development, and social integration*" (*Nurturing the Seed of Genius: Faciltators Workshop Manual 2009*).

1. Individuation

The first element of this theory, individuation, deals with orientation, or more correctly, disorientation or lack of orientation.

When we are born, we are like wriggling masses of electrical energy, with abrupt jerks, stops, and starts. It takes us a while to bring our parts into harmony so that we can make this body of ours work, and connect the head, heart, and body. As that gradually happens, we become oriented to our new world and slowly learn to navigate around in it. Our perceptions come into harmony so that touch and sound are co-ordinated, or sound and sight are co-ordinated. When we are firmly oriented to this world, we are fully focussed and able to use our intention to do things. We can see this clearly in the extreme focus of a very young child intent on putting a round peg into a hole, or looking intently at the face of a stranger as if trying to identify and categorize the object of scrutiny. Later on, we can see it in the rapt face of a child watching her mother make an icing heart on a cake and then trying to do the same thing—or even later, as we see a teenager doing back-flip after back-flip until the skill is perfected. An oriented person is fully focussed in the here and now, and his perception is accurate so that he sees, hears, feels, smells, and tastes what is really present in the environment.

If orientation doesn't happen, or is sporadic or unstable, we see the effect in what we call autism spectrum disorder. In a disoriented or un-oriented state, individuals' perceptions are not accurate, and they frequently seem not to be anchored in the real world.

Individuals on the autism spectrum are disoriented or

un-oriented all the time, or most of the time. That is why they so often do not respond in typical ways. Their perceptions are inaccurate, so they do not experience the world the way a neuro-typical person does. Ron Davis, who remembers experiencing this aspect of autism, explains this experience as that of living in chaos (R. D. Davis, Nurturing the Seed of Genius: Davis Autism Approach (TM) Manual 2007). He remembers hearing the ticking of a clock on the other side of the room and becoming one with the clock, unable to separate himself from the clock. Of course, the noise of the clock would then be extremely loud, blocking out all other sounds.

The boundaries between self and non-self are often blurred or non-existent. The over-reactions of many people with ASD can be explained by this sensation of living in chaos, because events that seem normal to most of us can be overwhelming to a person with ASD. I know of one young man who lives in a residence. He must be taken outside any time a cleaning person is going to vacuum, because the noise of the vacuum cleaner sends him into a wild panic. This is a direct result of perception being so inaccurate that an everyday noise to most people is a terrifying roar to one man with ASD.

This takes us back to the earlier discussion about USEs. Is it possible that the first cog in the wheel of autism is disorientation, which leads to inaccurate perception, and that other behavioural manifestations of autism arise from this?

This is, in fact, the first piece in the Davis theory of autism. Ron Davis believes that individuals with ASD fail to develop normally in a way that allows all systems to work together, so perception remains inaccurate for them.

Thus, the first step in any Davis program is orientation: finding a way to help the individual become oriented and stable in that orientation, so that she knows when she is and when she is not oriented, and knows how to get oriented quickly and easily if desired. When an individual is oriented, perception is accurate and the individual is aware of the true facts and conditions surrounding him. All Davis Autism facilitators/coaches are trained in various methods used to bring about orientation, and can identify the most appropriate method for each individual. Once that occurs and perception is accurate, the individual can begin to develop a sense of self as distinct from the people and world around herself. She has begun to individuate.

Davis facilitators and their clients work with clay to help clients learn (master) concepts, or ideas. Below is my use of a clay model to represent the growing sense of self that emerges during the autism program.

clay model representing a growing sense of self

2. Identity Development

Because individuals with ASD spend so much time in a non-oriented state, the extent to which they actually relate to the physical world around them is limited and often distorted. They do not develop sufficient sense of self to be able to understand the boundaries of themselves relative to the world around them. This necessarily limits their ability to interpret the world as humans typically do and understand their place in the real world.

Thus it is that the second piece of the Davis theory relates to this missing developmental step— that of learning about oneself and one's relation to the environment. Such learning is the primary task of children. They do it by listening, watching, touching, tasting, smelling, and experimenting. When perception and sense of self is distorted, learning is necessarily distorted. With accurate perception, the individual is now ready and able to gain an accurate sense of the world.

Based on this theory, the second step in the Davis Autism Approach Program is to literally draw the individual into the real world. This is accomplished through a unique combination of discussion, creativity, and exploration of the physical world. Through this process, the individual gradually becomes more familiar with the world as it exists, more comfortable with his place in the world, and more comfortable actually being in the real, physical world. As perception becomes more reliable and accurate, he can begin to experience the world as it really is. As USEs diminish in quantity and intensity, the behaviours originally developed to avoid or minimize the stress of USEs also diminish. This allows an individual with ASD to re-discover his relationship to the world around him. He develops an identity based on reality.

3. Social Integration

Given the limits of accurate awareness of self and the world as discussed above, it is logical that individuals with ASD are blocked to varying degrees from typical social development. In neuro-typical children, a strong sense of self begins to emerge around the age of two: a time we know and love as 'the terrible twos'. Parents who understand that this is a normal and necessary developmental step know that the child is becoming fully aware that he is a separate and individual person, and does not have to do what Mommy or Daddy says. That is why we hear the "No! I do it!" refrain from children in the terrible twos. They are trying to figure out what they can and cannot do. With patience and guidance, children generally pass through this stage, and move on to continue along their social and cognitive developmental trajectory.

Without typical development taking place, individuals with ASD remain stagnant in many important ways, failing to develop an understanding of how the world of people works, and how they fit into that world. They are, in many ways, locked in a pre-two-year-old, egocentric worldview.

With a stable sense of self emerging, the remaining issue to be addressed is the ability to relate to the other beings that inhabit this physical world. One of the key characteristics that defines autism is failure to integrate effectively into the world of people. Children and adults alike, whether severely autistic or displaying only mild symptoms of what was formerly called Asperger Disorder, experience difficulty in their social relationships and communication skills.

Based on this characteristic, the third step in the Davis Autism Approach Program helps individuals make sense of the world of people. As they become more aware of other people and how relationships work, they are able to learn how to navigate the world of people. Ron Davis believes that behaviour always serves the identity of the individual (R. D. Davis, Nurturing the Seed of Genius: Davis Autism Approach (TM) Manual 2007). As the identity of an individual begins to encompass an understanding of how relationships work, she is able to notice and emulate interpersonal behaviours without requiring specific instructions in the rules of social interaction.

I hope you will enjoy the trip 'out of autism' with me and the wonderful clients who have travelled with me along this path. As much as possible, I tell the story through the experiences of the folks who have allowed me to be part of their journeys. This trip begins with the orientation process and describes the experience of those clients who have sufficient language to follow basic instructions, and sufficient self-awareness to be motivated to do so.

Added bonus: My son, Desmond, has ASD and will be sharing his experience from the inside as we move together along the autism path. When he was growing up, I knew he was extremely hyperactive, oppositional, and dyslexic, but I did not know he had ASD. It has been an eye-opener for me to hear for the first time about some of the experiences he shares in this book. The only thing I knew that might have tipped me off was that we were almost never invited as a family to do things with other families. Des was just too difficult to have around. Because we never lived where we had family nearby, that meant we were usually alone for those typical family times such as Sunday dinner, or New Year's Day brunch. His contributions are clearly marked by being printed in a different font. He will also be able to tell you how the Davis Autism Approach Program helped him become who he is today— a fully individuated and gifted Davis Dyslexia Program Facilitator and Davis Autism Approach Facilitator/Coach.

SUMMARY OF THE DAVIS THEORY OF AUTISM

Autism is a developmental disorder.
Autism develops when an individual fails to

- Individuate (become a self-aware, oriented, separate person with accurate perception)
- Develop an identity based in the reality of the world
- Successfully integrate into the world of people and human relationships

The Davis Autism Approach Program consists of three segments, each designed to facilitate the journey of an individual with ASD through the three stages of development represented in the Davis theory as failed steps.

PART THREE
The Davis Solution: A Different Approach

1. Individuation

a. Orientation: Here and Not Here

There are a few methods we use to bring an individual into an oriented state. For those with sufficiently developed language skills, we use either Davis Orientation Counselling or the Davis Alignment Procedure. Both are described in *The Gift of Dyslexia* (Davis, 2010), and the most appropriate technique is selected on the basis of a Davis Perceptual Abilities assessment. For those who cannot understand or follow verbal instructions, we use an auditory orientation technique which involves having the individual listen to a specific sound (the frequency of focus), a 'ting' sound much like the sound of a triangle being struck, through headphones for several hours per day until orientation takes place. For those who cannot or will not listen to the 'ting' sound through headphones, Ron Davis has developed a device that can be attached by adhesive gel pads to the upper back of an individual which emits the 'ting' sound and helps to guide him gradually into a stable, oriented state. It is called a Natural Orientation Inducing Tool (NOIT).

Just because an individual knows how to get oriented doesn't necessarily mean he will like it or want to or be able to remain in that state for any length of time. A person who has spent most or almost all of his time in a disoriented state may take time to get used to the new reality. I believe one of the reasons our program works is that we allow as much time and space for the individual with ASD to get there as required. There is no *forcing, manipulation,* or *coercion.*

b. Self-awareness

Once an individual has become sufficiently comfortable being oriented and is willing to spend bits of time in that state, and is aware that he can wilfully enter that state when asked or reminded to do so, he can begin to separate himself from what is not himself. In other words, accurate perception allows him to begin to recognize the difference between self and non-self. In order to help that process along, a Davis facilitator/coach will have the client create a clay model of a person that represents the client's self. This process introduces the individual to three aspects of being human: body, mind, and lifeforce. A strong sense of self forms the base from which he can then explore the world around him, being able to experience the world through accurate sensory perception.

Individuation has begun when an individual can get into an oriented state for at least brief periods of time, remain there long enough to explore the world through accurate perception, and recognize that a clay model can represent himself.

Andy was 11 years old when we first met. At first, after he learned the orientation technique, he would sit at my work table with me for about five minutes, making little eye contact. Then he would turn sideways in his chair and glance at me quickly every few seconds as I continued to talk about the next concept we were going to 'master.' After about five minutes of this, he was finished! He would then get out of his chair and wander around my office and waiting room, talking non-stop and making weird noises. Every so often he would look at me and ask, "Guess what?" But he never waited for my answer.

After an hour of this behaviour, he would come back and sit facing me, saying, "What?" His demeanour and behaviour gave no indication that he was aware that he had just been 'gone' for an hour. His "What?" was my invitation to continue talking with him about a concept, such as *consequence*, on which we were working, and perhaps get started making a clay model to show the idea. When he had had enough, off he would go again, leaving me to try to make some sense of what I was hearing from him. Imagine my surprise when I finally got it! What sounded at first like utter nonsense turned out to be sound tracks from fragments of TV programs or movies, including all the music and sound effects. When he would be sitting with me at the table and go off, he often threw his head back and made growling, huffing noises. It turned out to be his reproduction of the noises made by the grandfather on *The Simpsons* TV series, who apparently often fell asleep in mid-sentence and snored loudly.

Gradually, the times he spent 'away' became shorter and shorter, and the time he was willing and able to work with me became longer and longer. By the end of five days, he was working with me for an hour at a time, and gone on breaks for about 15 minutes at a time ... a fairly regular work schedule.

Meryle, an adult I worked with, would often spend a couple of hours lying and/or sleeping under the table, or sitting on the floor in a ball, crying, up against the wall. As she got more and more comfortable being oriented, she was able to work with me on a consistent basis.

Raymond was a most interesting little boy. He confided in me one day that he didn't mind being oriented, but it was the 'smacking back in part' that he didn't like. He had a strong physical sensation of re-entering his body when he got himself oriented that almost hurt. He demonstrated by smacking his hand against his chest. The only way I can understand what he was communicating is to relate it to many near-death experiences I have read about. People describe re-entering their physical body as an unpleasant experience, understandable given that a near-death experience almost always seems to occur in a moment of physical crisis. They are moving from a place of total peace and comfort back into a body that is in the midst of trauma. While Raymond was not entering into a body in trauma (at least not in the ordinary sense of that word), the re-entry experience was not comfortable for him.

Bill was not autistic, but he deliberately chose to spend most of his time in a disoriented state. He even had a name for it. He called it 'dilly-dreaming,' and it was his favourite activity. His parents were at their wits' ends, because he simply didn't care if he was sent to his room; it was a perfect place for dilly-dreaming. He didn't care if he had a time-out because it gave him more time for his favourite activity. They could not find a way to motivate him to do anything except dilly-dream. The same went for his teachers, and he was doing almost nothing in school. After he completed Davis Dyslexia Correction and Davis Attention Mastery programs, we knew he could read and write, so lack of ability was not the issue. Working with his mother and teachers, we arranged that he would be required to stay at school to finish whatever work he had not completed during the day. They were to call Bill's mother and let her know that she would have to pick him up when he missed the bus to stay and do his work. That never happened. Once he knew there would be a consequence he didn't like, he got all his work done well, and in lots of time to avoid having to stay after school.

Colin was one of my favourites. He had an invisible car, and the minute he began to feel overwhelmed, his hands would go to the steering wheel of his car. He would become quite angry if he heard his mother refer to it as his imaginary car. To him, it was definitely *not* imaginary— it was invisible, but very real. There was a world of difference to him. I quickly learned to back off whatever activity we were doing or concept we were discussing the minute I saw those hands grip the invisible steering wheel. That was a clear signal that he was disoriented and not available to me at that time. Like Andy, he would wander around my office, talking non-stop, often asking me questions, but never waiting for or listening to my reply. When he was ready, he would come back to me, look me in the eye, and say, "What are we meant to be doing?" I would tell him, and he would get to it! Until the next exit.

Cam was also interesting. He spent most of his time watching and living in movies or TV programs. One of his favourites was *How the Grinch Stole Christmas*. He was accustomed to being told that he was too old to be watching that movie (he was 15 years old), but that made no difference to him. As he became more able to get oriented when asked, he would sometimes be able to do so, but sometimes it was really hard for him to pull himself back. He would sit across from me and say, "I'm ready," but by the time I said one word, he would be gone again. We might repeat that process 15 times before he could actually stay long enough to have a conversation. At other times when I asked him if he could get oriented, he would look at me as if from a great distance … looking the way I feel when coming out of anesthesia. It seems so hard to focus, and so enticing to slide back into that warm, cozy world! It was a beautiful experience when one day, as we were doing Koosh ball exercises (more on that later), he remained oriented long enough to catch ten balls in a row while balancing on one foot. He was counting out loud, and a look of real joy came over his face when he realized what he had done.

"Did you see that? I caught ten in a row!" he exclaimed.

I knew then that he was getting ready to inhabit this real world more regularly, and was feeling happy to be able to do so.

Cam's case highlights the difference between an individual with ASD who is not able to get or stay oriented and someone like Bill who is able to do so easily, but often chooses to be disoriented. My husband is another example of the choice element of someone who has ADHD, but not autism. He is a writer of fiction, and it's awesome to watch him write, often completely lost in the world he inhabits with his characters. He could not do that if he were not able to disorient.

Most professionals are amazed at best, skeptical as a rule, and downright dismissive at worst when they first hear about the Davis Autism Approach Program, and what little time it takes compared with most other autism treatment programs. I believe it is the orientation that makes the biggest difference. If an individual is not oriented when being taught, there is little chance of the learning being truly incorporated into his identity. Trying to manipulate or coerce an individual with ASD into learning or behaving just doesn't work very efficiently. Giving that same individual enough time and space to become oriented and to come willingly to the learning situation when ready results in meaningful and lasting learning. The individual is approaching the learning experience with intention and in an oriented state so that perceptions are accurate and what learning takes place will be accurate.

Meltdowns, or major temper tantrums, are frequent occurrences for many individuals with ASD. It is not uncommon for families to be held hostage by the fear of such meltdowns, so that family life is seriously curtailed by what the individual with ASD can or will tolerate. I believe these behaviours are the direct result of disorientation; the individual perceives the world inaccurately, becomes locked in his disorientation, feels completely out of control, and manifests that feeling through observable behaviour. The ability to get oriented and stay oriented for longer and longer periods of time allows the individual to tune in more and more to the realities of the world around her.

I mentioned Koosh ball exercises earlier. Koosh balls are little balls made of elastic bands, about three inches in diameter. Once individuals know how to get oriented, we do exercises with these balls to help them experience viscerally the difference between orientation and disorientation. The exercises are done while balanced on one foot, and the balls are thrown and caught over a distance of about eight feet. When clients are oriented, they can stay balanced and throw and catch balls, first one at a time, and then two at a time. If they become disoriented, they also lose balance, so it becomes an immediate learning opportunity.

There are two additional self-regulation *tools* that form part of any Davis program. One, an *energy dial*, teaches individuals to monitor and control their energy levels without medication. This tool is particularly helpful for those who exhibit hyperactive or hypoactive behaviour. The other, which we call *release,* is a quick and easy relaxation technique that is particularly helpful for reducing feelings of stress, frustration, worry, or anger. When used in conjunction with orientation, these are powerful tools of self-regulation which enable efficient learning and socially appropriate behaviour.

c. Coming out of the Fog

We will now proceed to see how specific concepts mastered in the Davis Autism Approach Program bring about significant changes in individuals with ASD, allowing them to begin to participate fully in life.

Mastering concepts is the technique used in Davis programs to engender real learning. In the autism program, we begin with discussion, talking with the client about the specific concept until we are fairly sure there is a beginning of true understanding. Once that appears to have happened, we then have the client make a clay model to represent the idea under consideration. Once the clay model is on the table, and the client has placed the word printed in clay letters under the model, we instruct the client to check his tools, meaning get oriented and make sure the dial is on five (or whatever setting the client deems to be appropriate to learning) and he is relaxed through use of the Release procedure.. He then looks at and points to the model and identifies it by saying, "You are (*word*) meaning (*definition*). For example, the client mastering the concept of change would point to the clay model and say to it, "You are change, meaning something becoming something else." He then looks at and points to the word printed in clay letters and says to it, "You say change, meaning something becoming something else." He is then instructed to make a mental picture of what has been created. This procedure puts a picture in the mind of the individual, or perhaps a new picture to accompany whatever picture was already there, and the mental picture, which includes the meaning, is what permeates the identity of the individual, becoming part of his identity.

Once that step has been completed, we go out to explore the environment to find examples of the concept in the real world, further linking the identity of the individual to the real world.

Self is the first concept mastered. The client creates four models depicting self. The first is a model of a person identified by the client's own name, or the pronoun "me."

(me: representing every experience "me" has ever had; all of the knowledge, all of the wisdom, and all of the understanding "me" has ever had)

Next, we address the three parts of a person, or what makes us human. For each part, we follow the mastery steps and have the client create models to represent his *body, mind, and lifeforce.*

(body: my physical form)

The exploration part of this concept is simply discussion about the client's body, playing around with what it can do, the different parts of it, and perhaps thinking about body parts other animals have that we do not have, such as trunks, tails, or manes. For young children, playing Simon Says is a good way to draw attention to body parts.

(mind: my thought process)

The exploration part of this concept leads to an awareness that our thoughts are only in our minds. We cannot know what is in the mind of another person unless he tells us. Our thoughts can be about what is actually in our environment, or about something completely different.

(lifeforce: my urge to be who and what I am)

This concept can be mastered as simply as getting to the understanding that it is the part of us that helps us decide what kind of person we want to be, or it can become deeply metaphysical when the client is an adult interested in such matters.

For the final mastery step, we have the client get focussed, point to the model of him/herself, and say to it, "You represent me. You represent every experience me has ever had—all of the knowledge, all of the understanding, and all of the wisdom me has ever had."

It is fascinating to witness the gradual development that often takes place in the models of self over the unfolding of a program. Sometimes, in the beginning, the self is little more than a blob of clay with appendages, but gradually it becomes more visibly iden-tifiable as a person as the individual's sense of self increases.

Colin was one of my favourites in this realm. At first his model of self was a little person standing on a mat. Each time he made another 'self' it went on a mat. I don't think he was aware of doing anything different, but the day he made a self without a mat to give it stability, placement, or security was an exciting day for me. I knew he was feeling secure enough within himself that he no longer required a mat to help his self stand.

Once a model of self has been made, we encourage the client to keep that model to use in subsequent scenarios. They do this at first, but it has been my experience that they will often decide to make a new model of self as their own sense of self begins to change. This can happen frequently throughout a program.

My son, Desmond, only agreed to do a Davis Attention Mastery Program with me at the age of 34 because he knew he was not being a good parent to his young sons. He asked me if I thought the program would help him be a better dad, and I told him I was sure it would. Keep in mind that, at that point, we did not even have a Davis Autism Approach Program, and I had no idea that Des might be on the autism spectrum. But I could see that his impulsiveness, constant frustration, and lack of self-management tools were making a mess of his life.

When we began, he would not make a model of a person to represent himself. He made a bishop, like the chess piece, and insisted that represented him because all his university friends called him "Bishop" (as a hats-off to Bishop Desmond Tutu in South Africa). I proceeded with that, because that is all he seemed willing or able to produce. We got all the way to the last concept, and he could not do that one. He followed me around the house for a few days trying to convince me that I was wrong, and that his understanding of, and model for, *disorder* was correct. We called a truce.

That made a big difference in his life, but there was still much work needing to be done. Several months later, he called me, saying he knew he needed to do the program again and was ready to do so, but he had a question first. His question was, "If I change, will I still be able to love myself?" I assured him that I believed he would be able to love himself even more for having the courage to change as he wanted to, so he came back and this time made a perfect model of a person to represent himself. He also completed the entire Davis Attention Mastery program. It did make a huge difference in his parenting abilities and in his life.

He explained to me that he had spent his entire life trying to convince himself that he was okay and was afraid he would lose that if he changed. Here is a poem he wrote as an adolescent that gives a poignant picture of how he tried to come to terms with his differences as a child.

I Like My Box Pink

By Des Smith

My box used to be red, just like
everyone else's except that my box was
sort of uneven. People got angry when
they saw that my box was different than
theirs. I think they thought my box held
less volume than theirs did, and
because it was just a little misshapen
they thought I was dumb.

And so my life went on in that
misshapen box, and it got redder and
redder. I tried so hard to make my box
like everyone else's. I pushed from the
inside, and all my teachers and
classmates pulled on the outsides until
finally my box was like everyone else's.

But then my box turned white inside,
and the inside was all misshapen.

Then one day one very special box
pulled me aside and told me that it liked
me better with my box misshapen and
that it looked cool. He said that the box I

> *had was very special, because it was*
> *different than everyone else's. It told me*
> *how to work with ordinary boxes,*
> *and how to cope with them. So my*
> *insides and my outsides came together*
> *and made a pink box: special, a little*
> *misshapen, and fun to be in.*

I LIKE MY BOX PINK

---

2. Identity Development

With orientation and individuation underway, we turn to the second, and largest, segment of the program: identity development.

Identity development occurs through the interaction of an individual with the environment. There are several theories about the stages children, adolescents, and adults go through as this identity development takes place. Essentially, identity development means coming to be who one is.

Erik Erikson's theory of development proposes eight stages through which people navigate as they develop. The first of these takes place from infancy through 18 months (approximately), and during this time the child is developing a sense of trust/mistrust as a result of the quality of care and nurturing received (Erikson, 1950). In the second stage, at two to three years, children develop a sense of autonomy vs. shame and doubt. To navigate this stage successfully, children need to develop a sense of control over personal skills and a sense of independence. The next stage during the preschool years involves developing a sense of control over the environment.

Piaget's theory of child development also sees individuals passing through stages, with critical learning taking place at each stage. His first, or *sensorimotor,* stage from birth to about two years sees children develop a sense of object permanence, meaning they come to understand that objects continue to exist even when they cannot be seen. During the second, or *preoperational* stage, up to age seven, children gradually evolve out of the egocentrism of early childhood to a view of life that can include understanding how other people think and feel.

It is not within the scope of this book to review social development theory, but to provide a glimpse of how that development may go awry in an individual with ASD who is not operating with accurate perception.

When an individual spends much or most of her time in a disoriented or un-oriented state, her worldview is filled with inaccurate information about the world. It follows, therefore, that the individual's sense of self develops in ways that are not consistent with reality, leading to conclusions that may not serve the individual well in the real world.

The second segment of the Davis Autism Approach Program is designed to lead an individual through the stages of development in an oriented state, so that he will be able to incorporate into his sense of self information that can be shared with the rest of society. It does not erase what identity the individual has already developed, but replaces faulty conclusions with more accurate ones. This is accomplished by leading him through an exploration of the world through the lens of basic concepts that most children learn and integrate through normal child development.

In this section of the book, we will be relating the Davis concepts mastered to the challenges of ASD, making the link between the program and the program goals of enabling an individual with ASD to participate fully in life.

These concepts are organized into three groups. In each group, or construction, there is a root concept, one that is considered to be a fundamental law of nature, or what Ron Davis often refers to as a 'God Law.' Each of these is followed by a base concept which flows from the root and provides an understanding of how we, as humans, experience the root concept. Finally, basic concepts provide further evidence of how the root and base concepts are actually expanded and played out in the real world.

There are thirty-three concepts that are mastered in the Davis Autism Approach Program. Each one is mastered in the same way.

We begin by discussing the idea, providing and eliciting lots of examples until the client has a basic understanding of the concept. For example, when we are discussing *change*, we might talk about how an egg becomes a bird, or a seed becomes a flower. We might talk about how a dry person becomes a wet person when he jumps into a lake, or how cookie dough becomes cookies when baked in an oven. We also get across the idea that change is inherent in everything in the world, that everything and everyone is always changing. We might actually make cookie dough and bake cookies to witness the change, or fry an egg to witness the change, or run water over our hands to feel the change.

Once the client seems to have a basic understanding of the concept, the creative part of this process is accomplished by having the individual create a three-dimensional clay model. These models always include a model of the client herself, so that it is clear how the concept relates to her personally. For *change,* the model must consist of two parts: the 'something' and the 'something else' it becomes as a result of change. The client then places a model of himself close to the change model so that the change can be observed by the clay model of *self.* The word *change* is written beneath the model in clay letters.

When the model is finished, the client completes the final mastery steps as described earlier, saying to the model, "You are change, meaning something becoming something else," and to the word, "You say change, meaning something becoming something else." Finally, the client makes a mental picture of the creation. Once this is done, we go out to find examples of change in the real world. At the beginning of a program, this step can be trying for the facilitator and the client, as we repeatedly invite the client to return his attention to the environment, while he may slip away into his own world every few seconds.

I well remember many walks with eight-year-old Alan. He would often bump into me, step on my feet, rush ahead of me forcing me to run to keep up, or suddenly veer off on a tangent. He would chatter non-stop about whatever jumped into his mind and seemed to be paying no attention to anything I said, except for rare occasions when he would suddenly make some comment indicating that he was aware of the concept we were exploring.

After exploration in the real world, we return to the table and revisit the concept in clay, having the client make what we call the 'simplest model' by following our directions, and completing the final mastery steps on that simplest model. Unless otherwise specified, the models in this book are in the form of the simplest model, skipping over the models created by clients in the first steps of the symbol mastery procedure.

a. Identity Development Concepts: First Construction

Root Concept: Change
something becoming something else

Change is the first root concept mastered. Individuals with ASD are often highly resistant to change, insisting that things always be done in exactly the same way and sometimes developing rigid routines for many daily activities. Change is the root concept that provides the basis for the first of three constructions in this part of the program.

One mother stated in an initial interview that she could never promise anything to her son, or even say, "We'll see," or "Perhaps," because if it didn't happen, life was not pleasant!

We work with this concept to help clients understand that we live in a universe of change. Change is happening to everyone and everything at all times. Once they *really* get this concept, their distress at change begins to dissolve. It took seven-year-old Colin a long time to accept this. I worked with him for a week at a time, about one week a month, for a total of four weeks. Each time he returned, he would walk carefully around my office, looking at everything intently, telling me, "I'm still looking." He was still looking to find something that had never, or would never, change. He finally gave up the search, I am happy to say.

The mother who could never promise her son anything in case there had to be a change was surprised by him six months after he completed a Davis autism program. She had to leave early one morning, so told 11-year-old James he would have to get himself off to school and lock the door upon leaving. He had never done this before, and it represented a big change from his expectations. As James' mother braced for the storm of objections, James calmly replied that everything was fine with him. He would just leave when his mother did, and walk another, longer route to school. He ended by commenting that there were kids from his class who walked that way, and he could walk with them. She was astounded that he was even aware of where other kids from his class walked, quite apart from his willingness to alter his normal routine, and to include interaction with other children in his plans. This incident was reported to me as a major developmental milestone, and one that James' mother believed simply would not have happened without the Davis program.

From Desmond

I was a planner. I planned (I used to think) because I was organized. Wrong! I planned because it was a way that I could control everything and everyone. The problem with that for me (yes, there were many) was that things are NOT in my control and because of that, things change. Change was my nemesis. A change in plans that was not thought of, initiated by, or appealed to me could and would ruin most things for me and anybody that was around me. There are many reasons for this; however, I will share with you what for me really set me on a huge disorientation and, some would say, "fits." I call it the snowballing effect. What I mean by the snowballing effect is something getting bigger and bigger–out of control. It would start with the smallest of things: a missed departure time; a dinner planned but the restaurant is full, and now we must go somewhere else to eat; going to a movie to find out that it does not start until next week, and now we have to pick a different one; or ordering a meal at a restaurant when you think you know what it is/should be only to find out they make it differ- ently ... oh boy! These are things to which most people just say, "Oh well, what can we do now?"

It was impossible for me to do that. For real, impossible. Looking back, I can only imagine what it must have been like to be around me when that was happening.

Let's take a simple thing like leaving to go to the cottage. Here is how it might have been in my house.

Remind everyone until they are exhausted that we are leaving *at 8:00 a.m. sharp tomorrow morning. Have everything you will need ready and packed today by 4p.m. so I can pack the truck. At 4:01, where the heck is everyone's stuff? Did they not listen? It is 4:02 and now dinner will be late ... GREAT! Come on, guys, get me your stuff. Oh crap, if dinner is late, now bath time and bed time will also be late. Now I will have to pack the truck after dinner, and now I can't go to the hardware store and get the darn batteries before bath time. Yelling now, "Where are the #*\$%##)*^^\$\$ bags for the truck?" At 4:03, "If I don't have your stuff NOW, then you won't be able to bring it." Kids are now crying and upset because they want to bring their stuff, and Daddy has just said "No." Oh boy, get calmed down and agree to wait until 4:20. It's 4:21 and still no bags for me to pack, and it starts all over again, only worse this time ... yes, it could be worse. The entire night is ruined (because of my behaviour). Now comes the morning of departure. It's 8:01 and we are not in the truck, I don't care why. I am still frustrated over last night's "change in packing time" fiasco, and that emotion carries forward. I really let everyone know that I am not happy. At 8:02. I am thinking "GREAT, now we will be stuck in traffic through Toronto; we will be late for our lunch date with friends, and we will make Mom and Dad wait for us at the marina because we will be late." At 8:04, "Can we stop at Tim Horton's for a coffee on the way out of town?" "What do you think?" I yell back into the house. We finally depart. I am a bear, unreasonable, mean and just not nice to be around. For the first 30 minutes, I drive like a wild* man to make up the "lost" time. Everyone is on edge and nervous and leaves Dad alone. But Dad just keeps going ... I can't believe that last night when I needed to pack and this morning, "Come on, guys!"

Change: it is a wonderfully simple thing ... now.

(change: something becoming something else)

Family Support

While a Davis Autism Approach Program is usually delivered by a licensed Davis facilitator, it is intended to be a collaborative adventure between client, facilitator, and family. The job of the family is to reinforce the concepts, helping them to become integrated into the client's daily life. This is accomplished by:

1. being familiar with the concepts by reading material provided by the facilitator;

2. using the language of the concepts with the client and relating them to daily life at home;

3. being aware of the progress of the client through discussions with the facilitator so that home support keeps pace with the program elements;

4. being alert to opportunities to reinforce the concepts, such as pointing out to the client examples of change, consequence, order, etc., or asking the client to point out examples;

5. creating opportunities that will reinforce the concepts, such as organizing a new experience for the family to reinforce *change*, or engaging the client in a task such as baking bread to explore the sequence of steps required.

One of my favourite examples of this comes from the family of a child with whom I did a Davis Attention Mastery program. The entire family embraced the concepts, calling themselves a "Davis Family."

Base Concepts: Consequence; Cause & Effect; Before & After

"I want my mommy! Get my mommy back here right now!" Alan stood at the curb, mustering all the noise and fury his eight-year-old self could summon up. I sat on the step just inside my front door, hoping none of my neighbours was at home. When I was fairly certain that my young charge was not going to run after his parents' car, or run away from mean old me, I pushed the door so that I could still hear Alan's frantic screams, but could not be seen by him. Sure enough, when I disappeared from view, Alan, still crying and yelling at the top of his lungs, came to the door to find me.

It had been six months since my friend first told me about Alan and asked if I would work with him. At eight years old, he had been expelled from a behaviour treatment program, being considered unmanageable and unteachable. A crack baby, likely also with fetal alcohol syndrome, he had also been diagnosed with learning disabilities, attention deficit hyperactivity disorder (ADHD), autism, obsessive/compulsive disorder, and a rare chromosome disorder. I had no idea whether I could help, but agreed to see him.

At our first visit Alan was like a whirling dervish in my office, never alighting long enough for me to conduct a brief assessment with him, not stopping in his incessant and very loud talking for me to ask him any questions. Eventually, my friend who brought him to me got him to sit for a few moments by issuing clear, direct commands—"Alan, SIT! ALAN, HANDS BY YOUR SIDE!" Her method worked, as it did at her camp for children with multiple neurological disorders, but was light years away from the gentle Davis methods I used. The only clue that I might be able to work with him came when Alan asked me loudly if he could give me a hug, after making eye contact with me for a brief second. Throughout that first visit he paid no attention to his parents, except to talk at them. He did not respond to their questions or requests, not to mention directions.

We agreed on a week for Alan to begin work with me, on the clear understanding that I had no idea whether I could do anything productive with him. We agreed that I might terminate our one-week program at any time if I felt the task was impossible, and receive no pay. If, however, we all felt some progress was being made, I would complete the week, receive my normal fee, and we would determine next steps. That was in November, 2007.

On the day in question, I had asked Alan's mother to leave. By then, I had established a pattern of working with Alan for one week at a time, and he was making excruciatingly slow, but discernible, progress. He insisted that his mother stay in the room with us while we worked, which I allowed on the condition that Alan could ignore her presence enough to work with me. His mother and I had agreed that if I asked her to leave, she would do so immediately, without any engagement with Alan. Hence his curb-side extreme temper tantrum. Until I asked her to leave, Alan's mother had been sitting quietly as planned, but Alan could not leave her alone. He was constantly all over her, trying to sit on her, make her talk with him, and do other things.

Once Alan came to the doorway to make sure I was still there, he stood outside the door screaming that I had to get his mommy back right NOW. He was not coming into my house until she was back. I calmly replied that she would be back to pick him up at lunch time, and went downstairs to my office, after convincing him that I needed the door closed. He would have to be outside or inside, but the door needed to be closed. He elected to be inside, so I left him just inside the door and went down the six steps to my office in the lower level of my house. He stood at the top of the stairs for another 20 minutes, screaming that he was not coming down until I got his mommy back. Every now and then I would calmly call out to him that I heard him and was waiting for him in my office. He finally came to my office door and continued to scream and cry, insisting that I get his mommy back RIGHT NOW.

"CATHY, DO YOU HEAR ME? I'M NOT PUTTING ONE FOOT IN THIS ROOM UNTIL YOU GET MY MOMMY BACK."

He eventually came into my office and stood in front of me, with tears and mucous streaming down his face, yelling at me as before. I asked him if he would like a tissue, and his response was to elaborately lick and suck the mucous into his mouth. I smiled at him and told him that was a pretty gross thing to do. He then yelled, "I'm going to gross you out so bad, you'll never believe it." He then proceeded to blow his nose and suck the results into his mouth. I smiled and agreed that that was likely the grossest thing I had ever seen. At that point, he gave up, got a tissue, mopped himself up, and sat down to work with me.

From the description of this experience, it must be obvious why a Davis Autism Approach Program is always delivered one-on-one. We go with the flow of the client.

As we worked our way through each concept, we talked about the concept, created clay models to show the meaning in a highly visual way, and then explored the environment to see how these concepts work in the real world. For example, when mastering *consequence*, after he had created his clay model, we went out for a walk to find concrete examples of consequence. We saw houses that got there because people dug holes, poured concrete, put up walls, installed plumbing, and so forth. In the park, we saw swings that got there because people made them and transported them to that place. We saw a fire truck, and speculated about what might have caused the fire to start, what might have happened to make the firemen get into their truck and drive off with sirens blaring, and what makes a truck move. The exploration out in the world makes individuals truly aware of their surroundings in a new way.

The next time I saw Alan, he had started hitting his mother frequently. As before, he wanted her to stay in the office while we worked. I told him that was fine with me, as long as he didn't hit her or hurt her in any way, because I had a rule that nobody gets hurt in my office. He agreed, and again I set it up with his mother that if I asked her to leave at any point, she would do so immediately without any discussion with Alan. Sure enough, about one hour later, he turned around and hit his mother, so I asked her to leave, and she did. We went through loud crying and tears, but nothing like the previous episode. At last, he tearfully asked me if his mother could stay after lunch. I replied that it was entirely up to him. He got a very strange look on his face and asked, "Me?" I said, "Yes. It is entirely your decision. If you do not hurt her, the consequence is that she can stay. If you do hit her, the consequence is that she will immediately leave, so it is your responsibility to decide." He looked at me as if I had suddenly grown another head, but quietly said, "Oh." And that was the end of hitting, at least for the rest of the week in my office.

(consequence: something that happens as a result of something else)

The next day, his parents had to leave to look after a business problem that had come up. Alan was not happy that they had a problem, but was able to remain and work with me calmly and effectively until they returned.

This is an example of how the concepts, once mastered, begin to become part of the identity of the individual, and therefore the individual can begin to think with the concepts. I cannot really explain why it works; I just know it does, because I see it happen over and over again.

As we work through this concept, the client makes many models. He makes one to show the idea of consequence with himself as an observer; one to show himself causing something to happen (self at cause); and one showing something happening to him (self at effect). The model shown above is the simplest model with which we sum up the mastery of *consequence*.

We also master *cause* and *effect, before* and *after* once *consequence* has been completed, using the simplest model of *consequence* and identifying the parts of the model to which the concept being mastered specifically relates.

(cause: something that makes something else happen)

(effect: something that is made to happen)

(before: happening earlier)

(after: happening later)

Together, these concepts establish a basis for understanding why things work the way they do. Because the models they make include *self*, clients get to create scenarios in which they are the cause of something happening, experience the effect of something happening, and also are in the role of observer. We will return to these three vantage points later in the program, but the seeds are well sown here.

It still amazes me sometimes how difficult it can be for some individuals to truly master the difference between cause and effect. As we explore the world, even something as everyday as turning on a light can prove to be very hard for some individuals to sort out. What is the cause of the light coming on? What is the effect of flipping the switch? Because those events occur so closely together in time, they seem simultaneous, and are therefore hard to separate out. Confusion is visible on the face of someone struggling with this, and it is a beautiful thing to see the clarity reflected when the light dawns (pun intended), and she finally gets it! As you can imagine, when an individual has difficulty sorting out the difference between cause and effect, the idea of consequence will not have much meaning and will not guide the behaviour of the individual.

Basic Concepts: Time; Sequence; Order vs. Disorder

Time is the next concept mastered in the Davis program. As we work on this concept, we consider time as measured by clocks in hours and minutes, and time as measured by calendars in weeks, months, and years. The definition for time we use is: *the measurement of change in relation to a standard*. Mastery of this concept therefore requires that clients understand the idea of a standard, something known against which something unknown can be measured. I often begin by giving my client a pencil and asking him to measure the table to see how wide it is. When he does that, I then give him another pencil of a different length, and ask him to measure it again. We can then discuss why it isn't useful to tell somebody the width of a table as measured with pencils, and consider what a better measurement tool could be. We then get out a few types of rulers and see what they have in common. This exercise, and possibly others like it until that idea seems secure, allows the client to relate this idea to the standard for clock time as the time it takes for the Earth to complete one rotation (24 hours), and for calendar time as the time it takes for the earth to complete one orbit around the sun (one year).

This can be a challenging concept to master. Its importance for individuals with ASD cannot be overstated. Time awareness and time management are often areas of great difficulty for them (as they are for individuals who have ADHD).

As we work through this concept, the client makes several models, again showing herself causing a change that is measured in time (self at cause), self personally experiencing change over time (self at effect), and self measuring a change taking place over time (self observing). Here is a model showing self experiencing the change over time. In it you can see the sign for free haircuts, the *self* with long and then short hair (change), the clocks measuring how much time it takes for the hair to be cut, and the earth rotating to show that this is the standard for clock time.

(time: the measurement of change in relation to a standard)

These are repeated for both clock time and calendar time. In a disoriented state, time does not really exist, or can be experienced in a very different way from reality. Lack of a sense of time or of any ability to manage time is often evident in the lives of people with ASD. The work we do in mastering time allows them to begin to experience the passage of time in a consistent and reliable way.

In the following model, the change measured is how long it takes seeds to grow, a change that would be measured with a calendar, not a clock. The standard is different, and it is the length of time it takes for the earth to complete one orbit around the sun. We call that length of time one year, and accordingly, all our "tools" (calendars) represent one year's worth of time. Of course, we break years down into months, weeks, and days, so all are represented on the calendars. You can also see the earth orbiting the sun.

(time: the measurement of change in relation to a standard)

The exploration phase involves lots of measuring of real-world experiences, or researching the passage of time for changes requiring longer periods of time than we have. We can measure how long it takes to fill the sink with water; how long it takes for the water to drain; how long it takes us to walk around the block; and how long it takes to build a house, a swimming pool, a highway interchange, or to become an Olympic champion.

When Meryle, a 26-year-old, completed the final mastery steps for *time*, she looked at me with an amazed look on her face and told me that for the first time in her life, she felt really grounded on this earth. She reported feeling goose bumps all over herself.

A week or so later, her mother called me to tell me about a significant incident.

She had made plans to get together with Meryle at a restaurant for dinner. As the time approached, Meryle's mother was there, fully expecting Meryle to be late. Her pattern was to be up to one hour late for any planned meeting, arrive with no explanation, and become angry or defensive if her mother made any comment about being kept waiting so long. She was in for a surprise. About 15 minutes before the appointed time, Meryle called to apologize! She said she was running a little late but would be there in 20 minutes ... and she was.

In his book, *Challenging the Myths of Autism*, Jonathan Alderson (Alderson 2011) speaks directly to the myth that if children with ASD do not receive treatment before the age of five, it is too late for them to get meaningful help. The information below about Meryle and her own report at the end of this book should put that idea to rest. Desmond's contributions to this book add further testimony to the powerful changes that can take place well into adulthood for people with ASD. Ron Davis, nonverbal well into his teens, has helped untold thousands of individuals with dyslexia, ADHD, and ASD. It is never too late.

When I first started working with Meryle, she always arrived late, often called after her scheduled appointment time to cancel, or sometimes just didn't show up. When she did manage to get there, she always arrived with food to eat, and frequently asked for some eating utensil, or asked me to heat her food for her. She truly had no idea that her behaviour would not meet 'normal' expectations for someone working with a professional whose time had value. I persevered because I understood that Meryle's behaviour was not really under her control, as she didn't have the concepts that would have allowed her to be more appropriate. I persevered because I really wanted to see if this Davis program could work with someone who had so little sense of time or responsibility.

Gradually over time, Meryle became more and more reliable in her attendance and time-keeping. One of her difficulties in keeping jobs had been her inability to get to work on time.

Sequence flows naturally from our work on time, because we can see how things happen in sequence in time.

(sequence: the way things follow each other, one after another, in size, amount, time, arbitrary order, and importance)

As we work through the concept of sequence, we look at it in five ways: sequence in size, amount, time, arbitrary order, and importance. Arbitrary order refers to some example of sequence that was simply decided by people arbitrarily, but then became accepted as a norm. The sequence of the letters in the alphabet is one example. I imagine there was a considerable gap in time between when letters were first created to represent sounds, and when the order of the letters was arranged into what we now call the alphabet. Names of the days of the week, or months of the year, are also examples.

While all of these are significant aspects of sequence, it is the *importance* one that seems to deliver huge returns. One of the characteristics of individuals with ASD is their difficulty shifting mind set once they have decided they want something, or want to do something. They seem incapable of understanding that NOW is not an appropriate—perhaps not even possible—time to do that activity. It is as if they live so in the moment that they cannot move off that thought. I know we are all encouraged to live in the now, but there are reasonable limits!

Mastering the idea of sequence in importance provides the framework which allows a client to begin being able to prioritize, so that when told, "We can't do that now," or "That will have to wait until after I finish the laundry," he can understand that, right now, there is another priority. This provides a good example of how the concepts flow from one into another, always building on what has come before. In the application of sequence in importance, we see the combination of change, time, and sequence.

Order vs. disorder

(order: things in their proper places, proper positions, and proper conditions)

The ball is in order because *self* has it and can play with it.

(disorder: things not in their proper places and/or not in their proper positions and/or not in their proper conditions)

The last concepts in the first construction of this part of the program are *order vs. disorder.* Order refers to things in their proper places, proper positions, and proper conditions. At first blush, this would seem not to be an area of difficulty for individuals with ASD, as they usually like things to be in order. But there are three aspects of these concepts that often are difficult for them. First is the idea of who gets to create order. In my office, I get to create order, and it may not be the way another person would like it, or even consider correct. However, I can create the order to suit my needs. Second is that there is not only one way to create order. People with autism, in their quest to create order out of the chaos of their worlds, tend to become rigid in their ideas of what is the 'right' way for things to be, and feel uncomfortable if their sense of order is violated. Third is the understanding that situations may alter proper order. When a glass is clean and not being used, its proper place is in the kitchen cupboard. When one wants a drink, the proper place for that glass changes; once the drink is finished, the proper place for the glass changes again. This idea of suiting place to situation is a big idea, and one that can help to loosen the rigidity of an autistic person's sense of order as being one way and one way only.

In the discussion phase of this concept mastery, we make it clear that the person who 'owns' the space gets to decide what the order should be (and why that is so), and from there, help the client to see that there can be many different ideas about what the right order might be.

Once this concept has been mastered, we can also begin helping a client to see how it applies to her behaviour. When a child is in trouble, it is always a case of disorder: the child is not in the proper place, and/or not in the proper position, and/or not in the proper condition.

This was important for 10-year-old Nadia. In her disoriented state, Nadia's position in space was often at odds with what I considered appropriate in my office: her feet would be on the table with the clay, or up on the wall. One day she broke the ledge on my white board by resting her feet on it, and we had a good discussion about where the proper place for her feet would be.

Nadia was also in the habit of frequently and spontaneously making very loud shrieking noises. That was disturbing to the other people working at my Centre, and was also problematic for her family, because she would do this in places such as movie theatres, restaurants, and at family functions. Once I was able to help her see it in terms of whether or not she was in the proper condition when she did that, she quickly began to monitor herself and modify her behaviour.

These concepts do not take root in the identity of the client in a smooth developmental trajectory. When Nadia and I went outside to explore the world, looking for evidence of the concepts, she would walk at an extremely fast pace ahead of me, so that I had difficulty keeping up with her, and, therefore, getting her to focus on the concept we were meant to be exploring. I teased her about needing a leash for her, telling her that she was my responsibility and that it was my job to keep her safe when we were outside; therefore, she had to stay with me. For the first ten days that we worked together, the best I could do was run to keep up with her and point out to her examples of change, consequence, order, etc.

She barely acknowledged me, and never pointed out any examples. I was therefore delighted one day while we were out 'walking' and I called her to come back to me and look at a garden we were passing. She did so, looked at the garden, and immediately said, "That's ridiculous! Those plants are not even in sequence. You can't see the ones at the back, because there are taller ones in front".

It was quite some time later that she came into my office and stated, "Cathy Dodge Smith, you are everywhere!" I did not understand what she meant, so I questioned her. Finally, in exasperation, she said, "You are everywhere. Everywhere I go, I see change and sequence and order. You are everywhere!"

"Oh," I replied, "You mean you are seeing examples of the concepts everywhere you go." She smiled in relief that I finally understood her. I too felt a great sense of relief and gratification. Nadia was beginning to be aware of the world around her and of the concepts on which we had been working.

In this way, the first group of concepts, or the first construction, allows the individual to become aware of the real world, how it works, and how he fits into that world. It allows the world of chaos to become a world of order, with laws that can be counted on, thus allowing the individual to relax more into that world and become part of that real world.

I don't want to leave you with the idea that disorientation is always a bad thing. In fact, the ability to disorient is what makes many people creative geniuses. It can also be employed in useful ways.

From Desmond

If left to my own thoughts in such a confined space as the back seat of a car with nothing to do, they would be relentless in haunting me! You see, I found the back seat of a car very similar to the experience of going down below deck in a small sailing vessel. If you have ever done this, you know what I am referring to. There is a sensation of movement, but your mind plays tricks on you, and you immediately feel unwell. The feeling of wellness returns quickly enough when you make a beeline back up the stairs above deck where your gaze can fixate on the horizon, and balance and movement return to a match. However, I did not have that luxury, and I knew that a long car ride was coming. Not only was it coming, but the last one and a half hours were over some of the curviest, windiest, bendiest, up-and-down roads you could imagine. Without being able to see straight ahead where the car was heading, I would spend the entire ride feeling like I was below deck in a boat. Yuck!

What I mean by thoughts haunting me is this: If something caught my attention, it was impossible for me in that back seat to let it go. It would drive me crazy. It could be something as simple as my sister crunching a candy wrapper beside me. And that would set me off. Perhaps it would be a stone caught in the wheel directly behind me relentlessly clicking away at anything less than highway speed. It might be clothes I was wearing that I did not feel comfortable in but was made to wear anyway ... rough, scratchy material with tags! I did not have the luxury of even drifting off into relaxing music (I later would find music on a Walkman magic). My parents were way too far apart from me in the generation gap for us to be able to enjoy anything together musically.

So now here I am in the back seat feeling sick and haunted and listening to anything from Zamfir, the flute man, to <u>Hooked on Classics</u>, and bored ... very, very painfully bored. What to do? You can guess what my behaviour was like on some trips, and how much I, along with my family, enjoyed travelling from time to time.

A thought ... magic ... that's it. This might save me and the trip! That winter for Christmas I had received a cool and unusual gift. It was a homemade AM radio kit. After it was assembled, I enjoyed countless hours of listening to CBC live radio broadcasts and hearing my parents, and sometimes their guests, laughing in unison to what I was listening to. I used to listen to <u>All in the Family</u>, hockey on Saturday nights, cartoons in the mornings, and much more. The point I am getting at is that I enjoyed those times because I was there with them literally: my parents and friends, the cast members, the audience ... everyone! I was in my room, but those times were magical for me as I sat under my covers secretly still awake in the company of all, but yet just me. I had a small tape deck. It was the kind in which the top *popped up and the keys were at the front. Stop, pause, fast forward, rewind, and record. The magic button—record. Could I use a 90 or 120 minute tape to record live TV? I wondered if I could recreate my 'under my blanket' feeling, but in the back seat of the family car. I promptly set up my little tape deck in front of the TV speaker (yes, only one speaker). The first show I tried was <u>Gilligan's Island</u>. I let the tape record the show as I sat in silence watching it. At the conclusion, I unplugged the tape deck, left the TV room, and retreated to my room. I plugged the tape deck in and pressed play. For the first 13 seconds, there was a hiss of dead tape, and then there it was, in all its wonderful power, just as I had seen it minutes before live in another room. I was recreating the experience of watching the show, but at any time I chose. What power I could wield! I could entertain myself anytime, anywhere I could take my tape deck, and it had batteries. The tape inventory began. I had multiple shows of <u>Star Trek</u>, <u>Bewitched</u>, <u>I Dream of Genie</u>, <u>The Flintstones</u>, <u>All in the Family</u>, <u>Bugs Bunny</u>, and many more. A trip that I used to dread was now a trip I looked forward to, because I could purposely enter a state of disorientation and live in my imagined world of TV Land. I would sit in the back seat, put my ear plugs in, and press play. Ah ... nothing but the sound of me and the TV, complete with commercials. Cool. My powerful picture-thinking ability made it possible for me to clearly visualize what I was listening to. The key was to record something so familiar to me that I knew what was happening when the Skipper was chasing Gilligan around* the island, or Samantha was chatting with her mother about what Daren was going to do. Not only could I 'see' what I was listening to, but I was there with the characters. Everything else just faded away and we all, including me, had peace.

That is just one example of when purposeful disorientation can be a wonderful thing. I have many.

Now let me tell you about a time when being in a state of disorientation led to frustration, public embarrassment, humiliation, and destructive behaviour to myself. The time frame would be the same ... 1978. We had arrived at the family cottage the previous day, and I was now out fishing in a boat with my older cousins. We thought we were cool because we were out without any adult in the 'big' boat, and we had a portable stereo on which we could play tapes. The music selected and playing at the time was AC/DC's "Dirty Deeds Done Dirt Cheap."

I was probably in a state of disorientation, just being a kid singing to a song, and suddenly I was shocked into the 'now' by laughter and a "What did you just say?"

I was being asked to repeat what I had been singing, so I did without hesitation, and with a sense of pride that I was being asked to repeat words to a song so that others might learn and join in, or be impressed that I knew the words.

So I sang in my best AC/DC voice, "Dirty deeds and the dun durn genie."

Laughter again, and a pause. "Say it again." So I did, to more laughter.

"What?" I asked.

"He is singing, 'Dirty Deeds Done Dirt Cheap'", they told me.

"No, he's not," I proclaimed (I had been listening to this song over and over obsessively since the release and acquisition of said tape). The mention of tape cassettes is important here. Why? Because cassettes do not have the CD jackets on which song lyrics are now printed. "I <u>know</u> he is saying...," and on and on I argued. I argued that position in a state of what I now know is disorientation so vehemently that I shed away two people that I should have been able to feel safe with for all time. However, from that moment on, I was always secretly ashamed and embarrassed about how I had behaved in the boat—alone, three young men in a vulnerable bonding moment. Thankfully, I only shared full time at our cottage with one of them. The other stayed across the lake with his granny and grandpa. It was bad enough when I was alone with the one cousin, but put them together in the same place, and I was sure the whispers that I heard were about me and how silly I was. I figured they had probably told their younger sisters and my sister about my

gaffe! From my experience with other kids, I already knew how vulnerable I could be when exposed out in the open the way I had been. I felt I was indeed the silly and stupid odd-man-out from then on. My emotions regarding how I believed other young family members perceived me were never the same, and I had lost the feeling of a safe family that I had previously enjoyed.

It was driven home even more clearly about what a complete moron I must have seemed to be when I returned home and went to a friend's house. My friend had that record, not the cassette. I was very eager to justify my position and set about putting to rest the embarrassed and shameful feeling I had endured in my gut for the rest of that vacation in front of those two cousins. However, that was not to be. The lyrics I argued so stupidly for were indeed incorrect. From then on, I knew that, when I was in front of the kids in my family, it was now going to be forever like the same ugly place that other kids lived in and haunted me from.

That particular moment in time was a life-forming and changing negative experience for me.

I will follow that story with this: <u>That's not Funny!</u>

Forward to September, 2012. I am returning my two sons to their mother's house after a weekend with me. In the back seat, my younger son is cheerfully singing along to AC/DC.

Yes, in this life I am blessed to share musical tastes with my two boys. He gets to the same line that plagued me those 24 years ago, and he says, "Dirty deeds the dun durf chief." Sigh ... and in a split second I am propelled back to that instant in the boat. Just then, I notice my older son starting to giggle.

"What?" I ask, hoping that he is not about to point out what I know he is about to.

He says to me, "I wish I could get that on video on my phone so I could post it on YouTube. That is too freaking funny ... 'and the dun durf chief.' It would get tons of hits."

I sigh. "That's not funny," and I tell him my story. Sometimes I think my older son gets the stories I tell him to try and convey the pain that I felt, but I doubt he gets it now at the level I know he will someday.

I stop and very clearly look at my younger son and, letting him watch my lips, say to him, "dirty deeds done dirt cheap." I give him a picture for what a 'deed' is and what 'dirt cheap' means. I know in my head that one of two things is about to happen.

One, he says "Okay, cool," and goes on singing and enjoying his music. Two, he says "Okay," looks at me, and at the earliest time when he thinks nobody is paying attention, changes the CD and tucks it away. I am hoping for number one, but sadly it is option number two. Inside I am crushed. Did I just do to him what they did to me? How could I have done that to him? I am happy to report that on my next visit with my boys two weeks later, I clearly heard him sing, "Dirty deeds done dirt cheap." He would not look at me directly, but I did see him glancing at me to see if I was watching him sing. When our eyes caught each other's in the moment he was singing that line, I smiled at him. The way he smiled back at me let me know that the way I had explained it to him two weeks before and then left it alone gave him the power to explore and listen to it again in the privacy and time of his choosing, and then he got it. Go, son! You see, my younger son is autistic and very much just like me.

b. Identity Development Concepts: Second Construction

The next set of concepts moves from the real physical world into the client's inner world of thought. We began with the understanding that we as people have three parts to us: body, mind, and lifeforce. The first construction deals with the real body and how it relates to the real world. Now we are going into the realm of the mind, and how an individual's inner world works. The world of thought does not follow the same rules as the physical world. In the real world, effect always follows cause; things are in order, or they are not. In the inner world, there is no time or sequence. One can change the consequence just by changing one's thinking. One can think about a car being totally wrecked, and in the next instant, see it as perfectly sound. Even so, there are truths to be discovered about how this inner world works and how it differs from, yet works in synergy with, the outer world to help us live a purposeful life.

Root Concept: Continue
Continue: remain the same

Now that we have firmly established the idea that we live in a universe of change, and everyone and everything is always changing, we upset the applecart by introducing the idea that things continue to be what they are. The definition of continue is 'remain the same'. Inherent in this discussion is the idea of life-cycle. Everything has a life-cycle, but during its life, while it is constantly changing, it also continues to be what it is. A chair will not turn into a table overnight; it will be changing, but it will still be a chair. A dog will not become a horse. This concept provides a sense of stability that is so often missing from the worldview of a person with ASD. It can also be great fun as we discuss what things could not turn into: a chair will not be a computer when you come back from lunch; that telephone will not be an elephant when you come back tomorrow. The model for this is simply one thing, an arrow, and another model of the same thing. This shows that the thing remains what it is over time.

(continue: remain the same)

Base Concept: Survive

This is how we, as people, experience the idea of *continue*. The definition of *survive* is, *continue as self*. We *continue* to be who we are: we *survive*. This gives the individual with ASD a sense of the constancy of life, even in the face of change. It is an opportunity to discuss how he has changed from the time he was born until now, and to begin to think about how he might change in the future, always still being who he is: being *self*. It sets the stage for where we are heading: the development of an individual prepared to participate fully in an intentional life. The model is a simple one of self, an arrow, and another model of self.

(survive: continue as self)

Basic Concepts: Perception, Thought, Experience, Knowledge,
Wisdom, Understanding
Perception: external awareness

Building on these root and base concepts, we can now take the client into his inner world of thought. This helps him begin to sort out not only how and why he thinks, but how other people might think. The first basic concept here, *perception*, bridges the gap between the external world and the internal world. Individuals with ASD are frequently so focussed on their own internal world, they are oblivious to the outer world. You may recall my description of Cam, and how difficult he found it to pull himself out of the world of *The Grinch* and into the real world. Orientation is the beginning of this process; now we are going to add meaning and understanding to the process. Perception is external awareness. We become aware of the world around us through perception.

We perceive when we use our senses in a focussed way to actually become aware of something that is outside of us. The model we use, and the first example we explore, represents sight, or visual perception. It consists of *self*, something outside of *self*, an arrow from that thing pointing to *self*, and a thought bubble attached to *self's* head with an image of the thing outside *self* now also inside of *self's* thought bubble. The arrow indicates that the thing that is seen outside of *self* goes into *self* and is registered as a thought.

(perception: external awareness)

Our exploration of the environment provides a good opportunity for clients to become increasingly aware of how perception works. It is not unusual for me to notice something the client has missed completely. It can then become a game to see who can notice something the other did not. The game brings home the point that just because something is in our environment does not mean we are aware of it. We need to notice it by having attention on it before it comes into our awareness, and therefore becomes part of us in thought. We can also try to think of things the other can't picture, because of not having had any opportunity to perceive them. Lots of my clients have all kinds of things they know about that I have no knowledge of, so we then have to look it up so I can perceive it: dwarf stars, obscure animals, parts of drum sets, etc. I get to try to think of things the client has had no experience of perception with, and therefore has no thoughts (or mental pictures) for when I mention the thing (crochet hook, Belgian endive, or a zester).

Once perception is understood, we extend the concept to the other senses and explore things we can be aware of through sound, touch, smell, and taste. As I was working with Carolyn, in order to expand her understanding of perception to senses other than sight, I used a lemon. I had her look at it and feel it. Then I cut it open and had her smell it. I squeezed some juice over her hand and had her taste it. She then got to squeeze it over my hand and watch my reaction as I tasted it, reacting to the sourness of it! Needless to say, we had to repeat that exercise many times.

The final step is a game in which I have the client sit with eyes closed and give him items to feel, taste, smell, or hear and try to identify what they are without the use of sight. We often have to repeat this game many times, as it is a great favourite.

One key component of discussion as we master this concept is the need for what is in the thought bubble to match what is outside of self. You may recall the earlier discussion about USES (unusual sensory experiences). We can talk about what sounds or textures bother the client, and why those same things might not bother another person. We can play around with perception while oriented and while disoriented to see the difference, eventually understanding that when perception is accurate, what is inside in the form of thought matches what is being perceived that is outside in the real world. Exploring and mastering this concept can be life-altering for a person who has hitherto spent most of her time in an inner world that does not match reality.

Thought: mental activity

The next concept, *thought*, expands the idea of perception to include anything that an individual thinks or holds in mind. While thought begins with perception, we as humans can put our perceptions together with our memories and imaginations to create limitless thoughts.

One important thing to explore here is the fact that one cannot ever *know* what another is thinking unless he is told. We can guess, but we cannot know. We can have fun trying to guess what the other is thinking about. This is hugely important, because one of the challenges for individuals with ASD is understanding that others may have thoughts that are different from their own. The autistic point of view is typically egocentric, making it difficult for an individual with ASD to understand others, leading to challenges with relationships. We will return to this in the Social Integration portion of the program, but the seeds can be sown here.

Another important thing to explore at this point is the idea of purposeful thought used to make sense of the world around us. We can observe people doing things and express hypotheses about what each person is thinking or doing. Again, we are bridging the gap between the internal world and the outer, real world. We can watch a person getting out of a car and hypothesize that he is going into Tim Horton's to get some coffee. We can see a person standing at a street corner and predict that she is waiting for the light to turn green so she can cross the street, and that she is on her way somewhere. We can see a person go into a drugstore and guess that he is going to buy something. We are leading the client into the realization that we can use thought to analyze and make sense out of the world around us. It is the beginning of the understanding that we can use our thought processes to learn about the world we live in, both things and people. The model is simply a thought bubble attached to *self's* head with something representing a thought inside it, and an arrow pointing to the thought.

(thought: internal awareness)

Experience: survive as changed

In this concept, we are leading the client to an understanding of how we learn. In the model, which represents a continuum in time (relating this construct with the first group of concepts, including *change, consequence, time,* and *sequence*), there is one model of *self* just hanging out; next is a model of *self* translating a perception into thought (incorporating his *perception* and *thought* models); and finally, a model of *self* with just the thought remaining. The idea we want to get across is that every experience we have changes us in some way by adding to what is retained inside us in the form of thought/memory.

(experience: survive as changed)

In the exploration of this concept, we continue the process of drawing our clients into the real world, with a focus on the nature of changes in *self* through experiences. One truly meaningful such exploration was with Veronica. One of her goals in deciding to work with me was to be able to go into a mall. At 16, she was not able to do so without having a panic attack and needing to leave. We were able to approach it as an opportunity for her to have a new *experience* using her Davis tools, and to see what the consequence might be. She was delighted that she was able to spend time in the mall with me, using her tools to remain relaxed and calm, and enjoy the experience with accurate perception. She was able to go into a store and complete a transaction with a sales clerk, and came away with a game that she really wanted. Being able to go into a mall is a crucial life-skill for a teenager, so this was a huge victory for Veronica, and she loved the consequence. She now has a new picture of herself in a mall feeling relaxed and competent rather than in a panic.

Once *experience* has been mastered, we expand that understanding into the different ways in which we experience life. Sometimes we are simply observers, as when we look out a window or go to a movie. Sometimes we cause things to happen, as when we make a picture for a loved one, or make a sandwich. Sometimes we are at effect, as when we are having a tooth filled, or receiving a gift. We have already planted these seeds back at the beginning of the program in the models for *consequence* and *time* in which self was depicted in all three positions. As we work with these concepts again, we are adding clarity and meaning to the differences. Ron Davis has chosen words to represent what we end up with as a result of the different types of experience. We are able to use the same model created for *experience*, making slight alterations to reflect the differences.

Knowledge, understanding, and *wisdom* are the words chosen.

(*understanding: experience of observing*)

Notice that in the model, *self* is simply observing what is out there in the real world. The arrow pointing from the object in the real world has been removed, so that *self* is simply observing what is there. Understanding is identified as what is in the thought bubble remaining after the real object is no longer in the environment. When we observe something, we gain a general understanding, but that is all. An example I often share with clients is about figure skating. I love to watch figure skating, and often do, so I have an understanding of how it works. I can tell the difference between types of jumps and spins, between good skaters and poor ones, but I cannot do it. This is a big concept, because many of our clients are confused about this and believe that if they have observed something, it means they can do it. They can be strong in expressing opinions about things with which they have no experience other than observing. They may exaggerate their abilities, failing to grasp that a different kind of experience is required before expertise can be claimed. Our exploration for this concept involves locating things happening out in the real world and deciding whether we have acquired understanding, or more than that. I had an interesting such walkabout one day with nine-year-old Cory. We came across a worker lifting building materials with a crane, and Cory assured me he knew how to do that. As we discussed the situation ... and it took a long time ... he gradually came to accept that he didn't *really* know how to do it; he had some understanding of how it was supposed to happen.

(knowledge: an experience of being at effect)

Notice that in the model, now there is an arrow between self and the object in the real world, and the arrow points toward self. This represents the idea that something is happening to self. It is fun thinking of good things that have happened to us, as well as things we did not like. The wording makes this a little difficult, because in the everyday use of the word *knowledge*, we can learn about things by observing. I can watch a painter painting and know how he applies paint to the canvas, so I have that knowledge; however, that is not the knowledge we are after in this concept. In this concept, we want to make it clear that there is a certain kind of knowing, or knowledge, that only comes from having an experience of being at effect. For example, I know a lot about what kind of knowledge people obtain from growing up with an alcoholic father, and as a therapist, I know I can help them deal with that emotionally. However, I did not have that experience, so I cannot say, "I know what that experience is like." That kind of knowledge, the kind we are talking about in this concept, is the kind that can only come from first-hand experience. The world is full of arm-chair experts who believe they know what they are talking about, when, in fact, all they have is *understanding*, not *knowledge*. We want to make the distinction clear through this concept mastery so our clients will move on through life with clearer self-concepts.

Nadia and I were out on a walk during this segment of the program when she had a wonderful experience of gaining knowledge, an experience of being at effect. She was a little obsessed with deadheading flowers, so every time we went for walks, she would deadhead all the flowers we passed. That included a large planter outside the office of a nearby dentist. On this particular day, as she was doing her flower thing, the receptionist came out of the office and exclaimed, "So it is you who has been taking such good care of our flowers. I have been noticing it and telling the dentist that somebody is looking after our flowers. Thank you so much!" Nadia wasn't too sure whether she was in trouble for touching someone else's property or not. She quickly realized that she was not in trouble. The receptionist then excused herself for a minute and came back with the basket of trinkets they keep on hand as gifts for children, and she let Nadia choose something for herself and for her sister. She then went back inside and brought Nadia a kit containing a toothbrush, some floss, some toothpaste, and some lip-gloss. Nadia was thrilled and agreed that she had had a great experience of being at effect; she now knew what it felt like to have a totally unexpected gift presented to her. She had knowledge from that experience. Of course, it was a great lead-in to our last concept for this group.

(*wisdom: an experience of being at cause*)

Notice that in this model, the arrow between *self* and the real-world object is pointing away from *self* toward the object. This represents the idea that action is emanating from *self* and moving outward; *self* is impacting the world; *self* is making something happen; *self* is at *cause* by taking good care of the flowers in the planter. By taking care of the flowers in the planter, Nadia caused the receptionist to be so happy that she gave her the gift. Now she has *wisdom*, the wisdom that when one does something helpful for people, they feel appreciative. At this point, we can discuss the things the client can *actually* do, and identify what *wisdom* comes from that. We can now have all kinds of experiences, and identify whether self is at observe, cause, or effect, and what is gained from that experience—understanding, or wisdom, or knowledge. Of course, we also discover that many experiences contain more than one of these aspects.

This is summed up beautifully in *Autism and the Seeds of Change* (Marshall, 2012):

> The words used—experience, understanding, knowledge, wisdom—are not new. They were an integral part of the recitation used to identify the clay model of self: "You represent me. You represent every experience 'me' has ever had, all of the knowledge, all of the wisdom, and all of the understanding." With the mastery of these concepts, the client is now able to fully comprehend the meaning of those words, to appreciate that 'me' is comprised of experience built of knowledge, wisdom, and understanding. In that way, the concepts learned will become integrated into the client's identity.

c. Identity Development Concepts: Third Construction

The first construction addressed the physical world and how the client can relate to that world. The second construction dealt with the thought world and led the client to an understanding of how that world works. These two constructions relate back to the first two parts of *self* mastered at the beginning of the program: *body* (physical world) and *mind* (thought process). This third construction relates back to the third part of *self* mastered: *lifeforce* (the urge to be who and what I am). It rounds out the identity by leading clients to an understanding of what motivates people to live life with purpose, and gives them the understanding of how they can live the lives they want to live.

Before we address the root concept of this construction, we begin by mastering what is most basic to life, what is necessary for life to exist—the basic drive that propels us from non-physical into physical beings and sustains life: *urge.*

(urge: the instinctual desire to seek pleasure and avoid pain)

In this model, *urge* is shown by two feeling bubbles attached to the chest of *self*. Inside one feeling bubble is a mini model of *self* holding a ball, representing the pleasurable feeling of having something wanted, and in the other feeling bubble is a mini *self* with the ball out of reach, representing the negative feeling of not having something wanted. The arrow pointing toward the having *self* indicates the desired movement toward pleasure.

Most of our clients are children, and children love animals, so this concept is easy for them to grasp. They are familiar with the urge that drives baby horses to struggle to their feet the moment they are born, kittens to nurse, baby turtles to hurry toward the ocean, and ducklings to follow mama duck. They are aware that nobody has to teach babies these things. We can easily move forward from there to a discussion about how that works in human babies who cry when they are hungry, cold, or wet (pain), and who suckle when an appropriate surface is presented to them, or snuggle when held (pleasure). This is easy to pursue as an urge that is in all of us to seek pleasure and avoid pain. We are born with the instinctual drive to survive.

From this basic urge, as we grow we become more conscious of what things give us pleasure and what things give us pain. It is fun to explore this concept by presenting ideas for clients to reject as unwanted or embrace as wanted. This sets the stage for where we are going in the third construction toward learning about participating fully in life. As Ron Davis puts it, "We are driven by our urges which are built into our lifeforce" (Davis, 2009). We are going to move along in the identity development journey to *emotion*, and in this *urge* model, we have the source of emotion.

Root concept: energy

(energy: the potential to influence)

In this model, we see something that looks very much like the model for *continue*: two clay balls connected by an arrow. However, in this one, there is a dominant arrow pointing to the connecting arrow. This model also reminds us of the model for *change* in which the connecting arrow means going forward in time. The concepts are being linked as we are building knowledge. The idea we want to get across here is that energy is in everything, but it only becomes useful energy when something is moving. There is energy in everything, so there is energy in a ball. But until that ball moves, it cannot cause anything to happen. Thus, the kind of energy we are mastering is the kind that is in a moving object when it has the potential to influence or to cause change. A wonderful example I like to show clients is a wrecking ball. As long as it is hanging beside a building, it has no movement kind of energy (kinetic energy). As soon as it starts to swing, it has the potential to cause significant change by hitting the building. In the energy model, the dominant arrow pointing to the connecting arrow indicates that the energy is in the motion of the object. But nothing happens until the wrecking ball actually hits the building, which is *force*.

Base concept: force

(force: the application of energy)

The model for *force* has *self* at the effect end of the moving ball, where energy is transformed into force. The relationship between energy and force links back to cause and effect. A moving object has the potential to cause change, but does so only when it produces an effect by coming in contact with another object. I worked with a young girl who loved curling, and she grasped the concept immediately due to what happens when a rock is thrown; nothing changes until it hits another rock. The placement of *self* ensures that the client goes forward understanding how this concept relates to him personally. It is not just an abstract idea, or one that applies to other people. This is crucially important as we explore how energy leads to a life lived intentionally.

Basic concepts: emotion, want, need, intention

(emotion: self-created energy)

This can be a tricky concept for clients to understand, although the idea itself is not usually hard for them to process; it can be harder for them to accept as the way things actually work. Our clients are not alone in this; many people find it hard to accept the degree of responsibility for their emotions that this concept entails. We find it much easier to give credit to the situation, positive or negative, than to accept that we can choose to feel the way we want to feel by choosing the thoughts we think. Ron Davis' conception of this idea is based on how the body works as a whole, with neuropeptides cascading throughout the body in response to situations and thoughts. He defines *emotion* as *self-created energy*, because that emotional energy is what drives behaviour. Most of us are not conscious of the process going on within, only of the way we feel in the moment. However, when we break it down, we discover that it is in fact our reaction to a situation through our thoughts about it that set up the *emotion*, or energy, we experience as 'feeling.'

In *Autism and the Seeds of Change* (2012), Abigail Marshall presents a full explanation of how this process works at a neurological and physiological level. A deeper understanding can be realized by reading *Molecules of Emotion* by Candace Pert (Pert 1999).

In the model, there are two thought bubbles, one representing *self* with a thought about having something wanted, and the other with a thought about not having the something wanted. Because there is movement, or a change from one mental picture to another (represented by the connecting arrow), there is energy in the thoughts. Because thoughts have feelings, that energy becomes a feeling. Thus, in the feeling bubble, attached to the chest of self, there is a mini-*self* holding (having) the wanted something, and a mini-*self* not able to reach (not having) the something wanted. Because it is a feeling bubble, it represents the feeling of having and not having, with the arrow pointing toward the feeling of having, the *urge* to seek pleasure. The energy is in the contrast, or the changing feeling as the thoughts are changing, so the dominant arrow points to the connecting arrow in the feeling bubble. If this all sounds confusing, it can be simplified by the understanding that thoughts are mental images; thoughts have feelings, but the thought precedes the feeling. Therefore, *emotion* is self-created energy. We encourage clients to think about something they do not have but would like to have, and put that thing into the model. If the thing is too complicated for the model, we encourage them to let a clay ball represent the wanted thing, which is what you see in this model.

How do we create the energy of our feelings? We create our emotions by how we focus our thoughts. Let's contemplate two people planning to go the beach for a picnic, and then the day turning out to be rainy. Person One thinks to herself, *Oh well, that will give me a good opportunity to shop for a new top and have time to read my book*. She feels happy. Person Two thinks to herself, *Darn. It always rains when we plan a nice day at the beach, and now the day is ruined*. She feels frustrated. This is an example of how two people can have different thoughts, leading to different emotions, in the exact same situation. That is how we create our emotions.

This is a particularly important concept for those individuals with ASD who often have meltdowns, panic attacks, or anxiety events. It helps them see how they can control their emotions by choosing how to focus their thoughts. What we are in the process of doing is helping the client understand how he can live intentionally, rather than reactively, to achieve what he wants, and thus learn to participate more fully in life.

As we explore this concept, we can set up experiments. I can set it up with others in the Centre that we will be exploring emotion so they know what to expect and how to react. I then coach the client to watch while I provide criticism to someone in the Centre, and note the reaction. We can then go back to *cause* and *effect* and discuss the effect my behaviour had on the other person, and discuss what she was thinking about my criticism. (Cathy is angry with me. I screwed up. I always make mistakes. She is always criticizing me.) We can then discuss alternative thoughts she might have chosen. (I will do better in the future now that I know what to do. This is a good learning experience. This will help me do a better job.). We also examine how that would have made her feel. I can then coach the client to offer a compliment to someone and observe their reaction, and go through the same discussion. We can observe people doing things and guess how they are feeling and what they might be thinking to lead them to feel that way. We can discuss times the client felt angry or frustrated, and what thoughts led to those feelings, and do the same for excited, happy, and delighted feelings. As we are exploring this concept, we are not only helping clients begin to recognize consciously the range of emotions they experience, but get the feeling that they are not victims of events and situations. They can, to a large degree, determine how they want to feel and focus their thoughts to allow that to happen. We are also beginning to make them more aware of other people and their feelings.

Jennifer was 13 when she completed the Davis Autism Approach Program. Her family was planning a trip to Florida, but her mother was worried, because Jennifer did not like to fly, and had previously had a severe panic attack in anticipation of a flight that was upsetting for the family. After her program, she was able to use her Davis tools to manage her energy level and get oriented to the true facts and conditions of her situation, and then to focus and control her thoughts (and therefore emotions) to control her fear of flying.

They had a great flight and a good time in Florida, with no panic attacks or meltdowns. Jennifer went on to become the valedictorian for her class upon graduation from elementary school.

Eleven-year-old James had told his mother that he did not understand what the feeling of *embarrassment* was. He had come across the word, but couldn't relate to it. She tried to give him examples of experiences that would likely cause that feeling, but he remained frustrated that he couldn't get it. Soon thereafter, he went away to camp for a few days, and he arrived back home desperate to go to the bathroom the minute he got off the bus. As they waited for his luggage, he couldn't hold it any longer, and ended up with a wet stain on his pants. His face flushed crimson, and his mother quickly said, "James, what you are feeling right now is embarrassment!" He was so delighted to have that mystery solved, he wasn't even upset any more about the situation!

Want: urge to exist as

(want: urge to exist as)

Notice that the model for want is the same as the model for emotion, with a change in where the dominant arrow is pointing. It is now pointing toward the feeling of having the wanted thing. The self now has the urge to exist as a person who has the wanted thing. Seven-year-old Marilee insisted that what she wanted was a mud pie, and she completed the rest of her models with a mud pie as her *want*. It worked for her.

Exploration of this concept is simply a matter of noticing people doing various things, and guessing or asking them what they want. We can also discuss things the client might want or not want, going back to the thoughts that lead them to their conclusions and feelings.

Need: something that satisfies a want.

(need: something that satisfies a want)

Each model in this construction contains and builds on previous elements. This model for *need* has one thing added. Outside of the person, there is the wanted object or its representative, with the dominant arrow now pointing at that object.

Until this point, *self* is the only real thing in the model. Everything else exists in thought form or feeling form inside *self*. *Want* is a feeling, existing inside *self*. However, when one wants something, for it to go beyond a feeling, one must identify what it is in the real world that, once one has it, will satisfy the want. This seems simple enough, but it turns conventional thinking upside down. We are accustomed to thinking that needs come first. We all 'know' that people must have certain basic needs met, such as food, water, shelter, and safety, before they can even think about other things they might want. I was silly enough to challenge Ron Davis about this early on in my Davis training, filled with my learning about Maslow's hierarchy of needs (Maslow 1999). He assured me that want always comes before need, and I challenged him again, so he gently asked me to give him one "need" that would come before a want. I replied, "food," and he gently told me that if he didn't want to live, he didn't need food. As usual, he was right.

This concept further links the inner world of thought and feeling, where a person with ASD often spends most of his time, to the outer world, a process we have been practising since we began. The intention is for the client to continue the journey toward participating more fully in life in the physical world, becoming a more self-directed person.

I believe this concept serves a valuable purpose besides that intended, of leading a person with ASD toward a more intentional way of living. The immediate wants of an autistic person so often seem to be all-encompassing, feeling like an extreme need, leading to tantrums or meltdowns if they are not satisfied. Once clients grasp the bigness of this concept, I think it lessens the grip of the extreme feelings of want. They can begin to realize that they only feel that feeling of what we normally refer to as *needing* something because they want something.

In our discussions and exploration of this concept, we can articulate lots of *need-want* combinations and point out that they are not always the same thing. If I want a bagel, then I need a bagel. If I want a drink, I need something to drink. If I want to lose weight, I need a diet that works for me. If I want a better relationship with my daughter, I need relationship-building strategies. We can watch a person going through a fast-food drive-through and surmise that the person needs food because he wants something to eat. We can observe a person going into a shoe shop and surmise that the person needs new shoes because she wants new shoes. We can discuss whether the person likely really needs new shoes in the way we usually talk about needing things (doesn't have any that fit), or whether it is simply a need required to satisfy a want.

Intention: the urge to satisfy a need

(intention: urge to satisfy need)

This model has a new feeling bubble, showing mini *self* leaning over to pick up the wanted thing. Continuing the journey toward self-actualization, the concept we want to get across is that wanting something and identifying the thing that will satisfy the want is not enough. One must actually do something to get or achieve what one wants, and that begins with the intention to take action as opposed to hoping or waiting for it to happen. The more energy there is in the *want*, the stronger the *intention* will be. Often in life there are conflicting wants, so the energy must be stronger to accomplish one's goals. For example, if one wants pizza, but has to go out to buy the pizza, an intention may be formed to go and get the pizza. However, if one also wants to watch one's favourite movie on TV and taking time out to go and get pizza will mean the movie can't be watched through to the end, there are conflicting wants. An intention will be formed to take action for one or the other, depending on the amount of energy in the two wants. This will take us back to the thoughts that led to the emotion. Whichever of the *wants* is thought to result in the best feeling is likely to have most *energy*, leading to the *intention* to satisfy that need.

As we explore the environment for this concept, we can observe people and guess what their *intentions* might be. If we see someone driving a car, we can surmise that person intends to go someplace. If we see a person walking into a medical office, we can guess that the person wants to feel better. If we see a person stopping at a red light, we can surmise that his intention is not to have a car accident or get a ticket. This provides an opportunity to understand that intentions can be about getting or doing things, as well as not getting or doing things. It is also a good introduction to the idea that other people have their own thoughts, feelings, and intentions, a concept we will delve into more thoroughly when we get to the third part of the program, *Social Integration*. It is all part of the process of becoming aware of the world around oneself.

This brings us to the end of the third construction. The three constructions were based on the root concepts of *change, continue,* and *energy,* and they led to an explanation of the world as experienced by the three parts of self we began with, *body, mind,* and *lifeforce.* We are now ready to pull these concepts together into a unified self.

d. Common and Advanced Concepts

As we have been building knowledge all along, we have been learning about the world and how it works at three levels. The first level was the root of each construction, a fundamental law of nature. These were *change, continue,* and *energy.* Resting on the root concepts were the second-level, or base concepts, those through which we as people experience the root concepts. These were followed by the third level, or basic concepts through which we continue to expand and experience the root and base concepts and discover how they work in the real world. The three constructions are shown below as three inverted pyramids resting on self, because we were exploring how the world works and how self fits into and interacts with those concepts in the world.

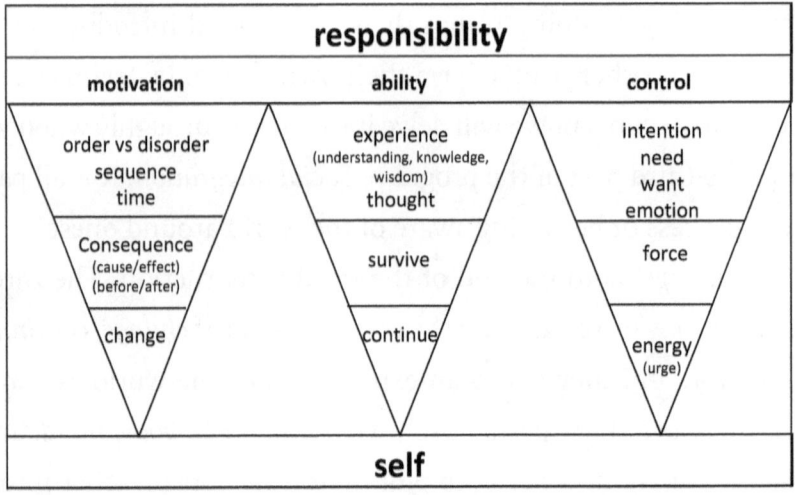

The common concepts link these three levels together in a fourth level, and each of these common concepts is based on at least two of the three root concepts. The three fourth level concepts are:

> *Motivation: urge to control*
> *Ability: knowledge, skill, and opportunity to control*
> *Control: the ability to cause change*

Motivation: urge to control

(motivation: urge to control)

Motivation links the *change* and *energy* roots, as it connotes the *energy* required for the *intention* to cause *change*. Clients love this one when they realize that they already have the model on the table! We simply remove the dominant arrow that was pointing to the *intention* feeling bubble. That action, and our discussion, makes it clear that *motivation* includes all that is on the table, not just one particular aspect of it. This provides a good opportunity for review of all the parts that go into motivation. Our exploration of how this concept works in the world involves observing many people doing things, and then guessing, or asking them, what is motivating them and what is the intention picture behind the motivation. It is certainly easy to figure out that a person going into an ice cream store is motivated to get some ice cream to eat, or a person taking a dog into the animal hospital is motivated by the intention of having his dog be well. It can get a little more interesting to think why a sign installer is working outside in intense heat putting up a sign and discover that he is motivated by his desire to get paid. This can lead to a discussion about why people sometimes are motivated to do things they don't really like to or want to do if there is a reward attached to the accomplishment of their task.

Ability: knowledge, skill, and opportunity to control

As we work with this concept, we begin by addressing each part of the definition separately. We first ensure that the client understands that *motivation* doesn't mean the job is done. It only means the desire and energy are present to follow through with some action to get the job done. Now we need to discover what else is required in addition to motivation to acquire the desired object (e.g. Marilee's mud). This concept links the first and second constructions based on *change* and *continue*.

(knowledge: experience of being at effect)

This concept has already been mastered as the culmination of the second construction, so at this point it simply needs to be revisited and incorporated into the more advanced concept. To do this, the client is guided to add another large thought bubble to his existing model of *motivation*. In the new thought bubble is a new model of *self* holding a ball, representing the knowledge he has acquired through experience, and which is necessary for him to be able to follow through with his motivation. There is a dominant arrow pointing toward this new *self* holding his knowledge.

(skill: experienced at causing a desired change)

As we address this concept, we want to ensure that the client grasps the difference between knowing about something and actually having a skill. Skill comes from practice, so in the model there are at least three very small *selves* in a small bubble within the larger bubble, each one in a position of bending down to pick up the desired object. The point we are making is that when we want to cause a desired change, there are some skills needed, and those skills are gained through practice. If one is motivated to knit a sweater, the skill of knitting must be acquired through practice. Only then will the individual have the knowledge of which specific skills to use in making a particular sweater, *skill* acquired through practice. Therefore, the smaller bubble within the new bubble is attached to the head of the *self* in the larger bubble holding the ball (or desired object). Now the dominant arrow is moved to make it point toward the three mini *selves* acquiring skill. If one has the motivation to visit a friend, one needs the knowledge of how to get there and the skill of walking, riding a bike, driving a car, or being driven. One can gain the required *skill* through practice. If one has the motivation to play tag, one needs the knowledge of how the game is played, as well as the skills of running and chasing, gained through practice. If one has the motivation to write a book, one needs knowledge of how books are written, as well as the skills of writing and story-telling.

Exploration can include demonstration of skills the client already has, perhaps drawing a picture, jumping, or playing a card game. Derek made quite a racket the day he brought his snare drum to the office to demonstrate his drum-playing skills, and gathered an appreciative audience from nearby offices! Exploration can also include learning a new skill, perhaps squeezing lemon juice from a lemon, making water turn red by cooking beets, or going into a store to carry out a purchase. Of course, we also explore the particular knowledge and skill the client needs to have in order to carry out her intention to obtain what is depicted in her model.

Opportunity: the authority, time, place and conditions to act

(opportunity: the authority, time, place and conditions to act)

Notice that the dominant arrow has now been moved to point to the object or ball at the feet of *self.* Self cannot pick up the object or ball unless one is there to be picked up. That is the essence of *opportunity. Time, place,* and *conditions* have already been addressed in the first construction in the concepts of *time, sequence,* and *order.* All that is needed here is to apply them in a new way to the idea of goal-directed activity initiated by *self.* That part of this concept tends to go smoothly as we consider the proper time and place for certain activities, such as brushing teeth, watching a favourite TV show, going swimming, or eating a chocolate bar. One needs to go swimming at a time when the pool is open; the TV show must be on, and one needs to be in the room where there is a TV at the correct time to watch the show (or at least that used to be the case before digital recording, Netflix, and endless reruns on the

Internet). There must be a chocolate bar present before one can eat it. These things are easily understood, although as we explore situations in the client's own life, it is not unusual to find that there have been problems over when the client is able to do things, or differences of opinion about what would be a good time and place for an activity.

The greatest opportunity for learning within this concept seems to be in the idea of *authority*. Many of our clients are not in the habit of accepting the authority of others where they are concerned. Whether this stems from lack of understanding the concept itself, or a lack of desire to please others does not really matter. Our objective is to make sure the client understands what *authority* is and why it is often important. One way to tiptoe into this concept is through the idea of who has *authority* over the things that belong to the client. That seems straightforward. However, it gets tricky when we consider whether a teacher has the right to tell kids to take their hats off in class, whether a sibling has the right not to share her belongings, or whether a camp counsellor has the *authority* to decide how loudly music can be played during free time. It sometimes is helpful during discussion to make a list of examples of *authority* parents and teachers must observe. It comes as a surprise that teachers are subject to a lot of *authority* of principals, unions, and departments of education. Similarly, children are often surprised to discover that their parents are subject to lots of *authority*. They can't drive without a license for themselves and their cars, they must obey the speed limits, and they must drive on the correct side of the street. They must pay for things before removing them from stores. We cannot go into a different country without proper identification. Just as mastery of *change* softens the attitude of an individual with ASD toward change in his life, mastery of *authority* tends to soften resistance to authority.

Alan was a child who did not take kindly to authority, and he was often noisy and belligerent when his demands were not met. You may recall Alan from the earlier story of his reaction when I asked his mother to leave my office. In the summer of 2009, Denise, director of a camp for children with multiple neurological handicaps, called me in great excitement to tell me that Alan had been at camp for 13 days without an incident. She also told me about one time when he went to her and demanded that she change the rules. His counsellor had told him he could only play with his Game Boy during free-choice time, but he wanted to be able to play it a lot more. Denise told him she couldn't do that, because his counsellor had the *authority* to make that decision. He was sure that Denise, as camp director, could override the counsellor, but Denise was firm that the counsellor had that authority as part of her job. Finally, Alan left, telling her that he hated that rule, but he went quietly back to his group and that was the end of that incident, as well as a milestone for Alan. At another time, Denise overheard someone ask Alan what cabin he was in. He responded, "I can tell you that I am in Cabin One and I can tell you that because I have that knowledge." *Knowledge*, *rules*, and *authority* are all concepts Alan learned in the Davis Autism Approach Program. It was Denise who first introduced me to Alan, and she was familiar with the language we use in the program, so was able to reinforce Alan's experience of those concepts in real-life situations.

We are now ready to tie these ideas together in the second

common concept, *ability.*

(ability: knowledge, skill, and opportunity to control)

With knowledge, skill, and opportunity, one has the ability to control. By removing the dominant arrow, we can see that all of the elements have come together to show the concept of *ability.* Because all the components of this definition have been mastered, mastery of this concept is easy. Time can now be spent demonstrating abilities and observing other people demonstrating their abilities. Derek and I were very fortunate on one exploration walk to come across a man operating a large crane, an ability neither he nor I had.

The third common concept to be addressed is *control.*

(control: the ability to cause change)

This concept links the first construction based on *change,* as control is the *ability to cause change,* with the second construction based on continue, which contains the *knowledge, skill,* and *opportunity* as a necessary prerequisite for effective action. All of the components are already in the model on the table. All the client needs to do is make the connection that *self* now has everything required to take action and to show that in the model. Real *self* (not *self*-contained within a thought or feeling bubble) must lean down and pick up the object to demonstrate *control.* The dominant arrow now points toward *self* picking up the object. Once that concept is clear, time can be spent observing people taking *control* through action and having the client demonstrate herself exercising *control* through action. It is useful to review all the things the client has already done just in that day that demonstrate *control*: got out of bed, got dressed, put on boots or shoes, put on jacket, got into a car, opened doors, ate breakfast. Then we can think of new things to do to practise *control.*

Responsibility

We are now truly ready to pull all the concepts together with the final, fifth level Advanced Concept: *responsibility.* Through this concept, the parallel identity we have been building is pulled together to be integrated within the identity of the individual. The effect of this is that the parallel identity and all the concepts built into it will influence all future thoughts and behaviours of the individual. It is a process of adding to the knowledge, wisdom, and understanding of the individual rather than simply teaching new behaviours. Thus, the individual is ready and able to make his own choices about future behaviours based on a solid and accurate understanding of how things work.

(responsibility: motivation and ability to control)

Notice that in the model, the only change is that *self* now is holding the object or ball, and the dominant arrow pointing to *self* picking up the ball is now gone. The goal has been accomplished. Responsibility links all three root concepts by pulling motivation and ability together. What it means is that one must have motivation *and* ability to be responsible. In other words, one must be willing and able to do something in order to be responsible. If one is responsible for keeping the family garden looking nice, that means one must be motivated (willing) and able to do so. If a person is not willing, she will not do it, and will not be responsible for it. If she is willing but not able, she will not get it done, and, therefore, not be responsible.

Most individuals with autism have had little experience with responsibility, largely because the nature of autism makes taking responsibility for things very difficult. Taking responsibility requires having a clear understanding of what is to be accomplished and how one can go about doing so. When one is disoriented most of the time, one cannot also be aware of the true conditions in the environment, or have a clear understanding of the situation. Therefore, understanding what is required and being able to carry out the requirements is challenging. Having no, or a poor, grasp of the concept of *consequence* makes it challenging for an individual to figure out what to do to bring about the desired result. Failure to understand *sequence* makes it difficult to figure out the sequence of steps necessary to even make a sandwich, let alone tidy up afterward.

What happens then is that the individual with ASD is either constantly being chastised for not living up to his responsibilities (for pet caring, doing homework, sharing, behaving appropriately in public, or getting dressed in a timely manner in the morning), or he is not expected to take responsibility for such tasks because his family has given up expectations. In either case, being responsible is not something with which most people with ASD are familiar.

Discussion of this concept unfailingly brings up many situations the client is aware of in which she is not living up to expectations—hers or other people's. Discussion begins with examination of which factor is missing: motivation or ability. Parents and teachers often assume *motivation* is missing regarding school work. However, on close examination, it turns out there is some part of the task that the client is not able to do independently. Once individuals understand this concept, they are empowered to analyze a situation and make logical decisions about whether they are willing to be responsible for a particular task, or whether they need help to be able to do so. This is a very important step toward becoming a responsible individual, able to make choices and live an intentional (goal-directed) life.

One example involves nine-year-old Nadia as mentioned previously. Her family was stressed because they felt they could not go to public places, such as movies or restaurants, as a family, because Nadia would frequently let out very loud shrieks. As I worked with her, she did so frequently in my office setting. Once she understood cause and effect and was able to process the effect her noise had on other people as they were trying to work, we were able to work on that behaviour. I also insisted that we return to my office and close the door every time she made that loud noise, so she became aware that there would be consequences every time she made that noise. It took a short amount of time for her to learn not to shriek in public places. What was lacking in that situation was motivation, but the lack of motivation was caused by her lack of knowledge and understanding. With understanding, she was quickly willing and able to change her behavior. Now she behaves 'responsibly' in public places.

With *responsibility,* we have finished the Identity Development part of the program. The program has been *uploaded,* to use Ron Davis' terminology and computer software analogy. We then do three exercises to ensure that the concepts mastered are operational within the individual. Now it is time to *run* the program. We have the client engage in three exercises to put into action being responsible for a task. This step involves having the client first establish order with a jigsaw puzzle, then with items from the immediate environment, and finally in the client's own home environment in some area for which he is willing to take responsibility. These exercises set the program in motion, so that all future thoughts and behaviours will run through the client's new parallel identity based on the concepts.

Derek's story provides an amusing example of how this can work. We finished *responsibility,* and the first two order exercises, with 10-year-old Derek on a Thursday, but didn't have the opportunity to go to his home before his family went away for the weekend. However, he had told me in no uncertain terms that his room was a total mess, and he didn't want to change that. His mother emailed me the day after their return to tell me that Derek had a very interesting reaction when they got home from their cottage weekend. He declared that his room was in disorder and he didn't want to sleep in it until it was in order, so they worked until 10:00 p.m. that evening establishing order in his room!

Marilee had a more difficult time. On the appointed day, I went to Marilee's house to help her establish order. She decided she wanted to establish order in the basement playroom. Her mother tried to redirect her to her bedroom, saying that the basement was too big a job. The family had been in some construction turmoil and no tidying had been done in the basement for quite some time. Marilee was insistent that she wanted to work on the basement and would not be dissuaded. When I went down to have a look with her, I again tried to persuade her to choose someplace less daunting, but she was adamant, so we got started. She worked with me for about 20 minutes and was then ready for a break. Off she went to play while her mother and I chatted. When it was time to get back to work, Marilee announced that she didn't want to do it any more.

One of Marilee's parents' goals regarding my work with Marilee was for them to learn better ways of parenting her and her sister. Marilee was an extremely headstrong young eight-year-old and often seemed to rule the household. This seemed to be a good time to address Marilee's behaviour, now that she had a good understanding of cause and effect. It was also a good opportunity for her mother to practise the new method of parenting she wanted to learn. Before this, everyone in the house would end up in a very upset state when Marilee didn't get her way.

I explained to Marilee that, because she didn't listen to her mother or me but insisted on choosing the basement in which to establish order, the task seemed harder and was taking longer than it would have otherwise, but it had been her choice, so now her job was to complete the task. Her mother explained that, as I had come to her house to help her establish order, it was Marilee's job to cooperate with me. Marilee was having none of it. I suggested to her mother that this would be an appropriate time to use the Supernanny technique of parenting,[2] in which I had already coached her and for which I had provided support materials. Accordingly, Marilee's mother gave her a choice: to cooperate, or to have a time-out. She refused to co-operate, so her mother took her to a time-out spot and used the Supernanny dialogue. For over two hours, Marilee yelled, cried, threw a full-on tantrum, threw things, and repeatedly left her spot. With guidance, her mother kept putting her back until she finally gave in, apologized, and came back to work. In the meantime, her mother and I continued

---

2   The Supernanny parenting techniques are not part of a Davis program, but parents often request help in establishing new patterns of parenting after their child has completed a Davis concept-based program. The Supernanny methods are relatively easy to learn and apply and fit well within the framework of the Davis concepts. In the Supernanny paradigm, children are provided with clear expectations about what is considered acceptable and not acceptable behaviour within the family. If they behave in a way that is not considered acceptable by the family, they are given one warning to change the behaviour. If they do not change (stop doing something, or start doing something), they are given a time-out reflecting one minute for each year of the child's age. At the end of the time-out, meaning that the child has actually stayed in the established 'naughty spot' for the designated time, the child is reminded why he was there and asked to apologize. If he does, he gets a hug and is invited to now do/not do whatever the triggering behaviour was. If he complies, that is the end of it. There is no further discussion. If he refuses, he gets another time-out. There is still no further discussion. This is a very rudimentary explanation of the technique. For more information, look for books by Jo Frost, or go to her web site at www.jofrost.com.

to chat and laugh, demonstrating to Marilee that her tantrum was upsetting her, but nobody else. This was hard for the mom, but a good lesson for her in stress-free parenting. When Marilee was ready to come back to work, she settled in happily and was finished in 15 minutes. We then sat on the floor and played a game together.

This experience marked a positive turning point for Marilee and her family. It gave her mother the technique and confidence to set boundaries for Marilee and stick to them without any anger or frustration on her part. It gave Marilee a clear message that there would be consequences for her unacceptable behaviour, and that her mother was, in a sense, taking back her parenting role—exercising her *authority*. It also activated the entire cascade of concepts in Marilee, ensuring that she was aware of her role in the consequences that came her way and that she could make choices leading to positive consequences if that was what she wanted.

It is important that the child have mastered the concepts *before* this parenting technique is instigated. If the child does not have a good understanding of consequence and order vs. disorder, attempts to get her to comply with family rules are likely to be met with great resistance and result in the child feeling picked on or unfairly treated. Once the concepts are in place, the child can understand and make sense of the experience of facing consequences for her behaviour.

3. Social Integration

All of the concepts we have been working with in the identity development segment of this program have been about the world: how the world works and how the client fits into the world. As a person with ASD progresses through the concepts and becomes more aware of his surroundings, greater awareness of other people begins to take place. Part of this happens naturally as the client becomes more oriented for longer periods of time. Simply put, the client is fully present, aware of the true facts and conditions of his environment more frequently. Because his environment includes people, he naturally becomes more aware of other people. During our explorations of the concepts, we naturally pay attention to the people in the environment. For example, the day Nadia was given gifts by the dentist's administrator, she was aware of the other person involved. We set up experiments and 'notice' other peoples' reactions at various points.

In the third segment of the program, we address the world of people and relationships head-on. Clients are helped to understand that just as they have thoughts, emotions, wants, needs, intentions, knowledge, skills, and abilities, so do other people.

There are three sections to this segment of the Davis Autism Approach. The first simply introduces the idea that there are other people in the world and we interact with them one at a time, or in groups. The second introduces the idea of relationships and looks at how relationships are established and maintained: what makes them work well and what makes them work not so well. The third and last part provides some guidance into how to make decisions, providing the basis of a conscience to guide the decisions and behaviours of the client going forward.

The concepts for this segment are:

Another: individual separate from self
Others: individuals separate from self

Behaviour: how one acts or conducts oneself
Emotion: self-created energy

Relationship: interaction of one with another
Trust: the feeling that another is equal to self
Belief: what we feel is actual or real
Agree: what we think is actual or real
Rules: regulations that establish boundaries of acceptable behaviour

Bad: not in support of survival
Good: in support of survival
Wrong: an action not in support of survival
Right: an action in support of survival

(another: individual separate from self)

This model is very simple: *self* and one *other* person, with the arrow pointing to the *other*. The idea we want to get across is that there are other people in this time-space reality world, and they are just like *self* in that they also have all the attributes we have been applying to self. They have their own interests, wants, needs, intentions, experiences, abilities, and responsibilities. While this seems like a simple concept, it can be huge for an individual who has been accustomed to viewing the world from an egocentric perspective, and that is one of the defining characteristics of autism. People with autism often are not aware of other people in their environments except as directly related to them, and most specifically when *another* seems to be thwarting their desires. This perspective is similar to what is seen in very young children who see the world from their own vantage point. *Another* is 'nice' if doing his will, and 'mean' if not. It is common to hear toddlers telling their parents that they hate them or that they are mean. What they mean is, "You are not doing what I want you to do right now." They do not consider that there could be a good reason for the behaviour of the *other*. Putting *self* in another's shoes is not part of the package.

I like to begin this section of the program by discussing the difference between social animals and solitary animals. Most of my clients love animals and they are either familiar with this idea, or grasp it easily when given examples. Bears, leopards, and crocodiles live by themselves, so we call them solitary animals. Elephants, wolves, and caribou live in groups called herds or packs, so we call them social animals. Many children with ASD prefer watching documentaries to other forms of TV entertainment, so this is familiar territory to them. We can easily segue into the idea of people as social animals. We live and work and play in groups, not usually alone.

The exploration portion of this part of the program is different from what we have been doing in the Identity Development segment. What we are now doing is laying the groundwork for thinking about other people objectively rather than subjectively, and establishing relationships with them. Rather than going out to explore the world in this segment, we discuss the concept, relating it to previous experiences and to some of the other concepts we have already mastered, trusting that insight will ensue and continue.

When discussing *another*, we might review many of the concepts already mastered, such as *want*, *need*, *emotion*, *intention*, and *experience*, and discuss how these might apply to individuals well known to the client. For example, if the client thinks parents are not reasonable about things like bedtime, time allowed on electronic devices, or family food regulations, we might ask him to think about what the intentions of his parents might be. If the client believes school rules are stupid we might ask her what she thinks the intentions of the teacher or principal might be. These discussions can often provide insights to the clients that were not experienced previously. This is not a time for the facilitator to teach, but rather to provide opportunities for clients to think. A discussion about *responsibility* regarding *another* can lead a client to a new understanding of responsibilities his parents have that could interfere with what the client wants.

One of the behaviours I have frequently noted in clients with ASD is extreme invasion of another's space. Children will often take their parent's face in their hands, trying to force the parent to look at the child and put his own face right up to the face of the parent, touching it with his own if the parent is not paying attention to the child at that moment. Clients often drape themselves over a parent while the parent and I are trying to have a conversation. This behaviour diminishes once the child has a clear sense of *another* as separate from *self*.

Interrupting is one of the bothersome behaviours I hear about a great deal from parents. When children interrupt, it means they want attention and have no sense that the person from whom they are seeking attention might be doing something important to that person. All the interrupter knows is that he has something important to say and has no sense that the parent might not want to listen at that moment. If the parent does not respond immediately, the child becomes insistent, continuing to interrupt, perhaps using his body to try to force the parent to listen as described above.

The TV sitcom *Big Bang Theory* presents a gently humourous perspective on autism. For example, the main character, Sheldon, insists on sitting in his own spot, even if someone else is already sitting there when he enters the room. He insists that nobody in his environment should watch a TV show he doesn't like. These are examples of failure truly to recognize another as an individual separate from oneself.

Before we got to the Social Integration part of the program, Colin and I were making up scenarios for a game designed to teach positive social attitudes. The game is similar to the Monopoly game, except the instruction cards have scenarios, each of which has a positive attitude reaction and a negative attitude reaction. The roll of the die decides which attitude the player 'chooses' with a positive consequence for a positive attitude and negative consequence for a negative attitude. A typical scenario would be: You agreed to feed, brush, walk, and clean up after the dog before you got a puppy. Today you didn't walk the puppy in time and the puppy made a mess. Positive attitude is: "You know the puppy is your responsibility. You clean up the mess." Negative attitude is: "You know that if you wait long enough, your mum will clean it up." The player then gets to move forward if his attitude is positive, or has a penalty if his attitude is negative.

Colin loved the game and enjoyed making up new scenarios to add to the game. At one point, it was my turn to make up a new scenario. I began, "You are playing with your younger brother when ..." He told me that I couldn't write that down because he didn't have a younger brother. No matter how I tried to explain that these scenarios were for all children who might play the game and some might have younger brothers, he remained adamant that *he* didn't have a younger brother, so it couldn't be in the game.

This would be quite typical of a child with ASD before mastering the Social Integration concepts. Colin's teacher came to meet with me during the time I worked with him. She told me that she thought he was able to empathize, so doubted that he was autistic. For an example, she told me that once when they were having a movie day at school, they ran out of popcorn and Colin gave his to one of the kids who didn't get any, saying, "You can have mine. I don't like popcorn." I asked what she thought Colin would have done if he had wanted his popcorn, and she got it.

(others: individuals separate from self)

This model simply adds several more *others* to the table. Mastery and discussion provide an opportunity to explore the idea that sometimes we interact with one other person at a time and sometimes with groups of other people. Sometimes there may be one other person in the environment and sometimes more than one other. Playing with one person is different from being in a group of people, whether at school, in sports, in lessons, or even at home. Sometimes the *others* belong to a group with which we are interacting, as when we are at school, in church, at Scouts, in gym class, or at camp. Sometimes the *others* are simply in our environment, but not interacting with us in a group format. This could be when we are at the beach, walking down a street, in a mall, or at a park.

Discussion of *others* provides a good time to introduce the idea of group norms or expectations. When I am at choir practice, that is not an appropriate time for me to tell jokes to the person sitting beside me. All of us are there to sing, so the appropriate behaviour is to listen to the director and do what he says. When the client's teacher is speaking to the class, that is a time for all students to listen, not to talk to each other, or make distracting noises.

Derek was very upset and angry that kids at school were making fun of him because he sucked his thumb and always took a very large stuffed animal to school with him. This consideration of *others* gave us the opportunity to discuss what other kids his age did and did not do at school. Sucking thumbs and carrying stuffies around was in the 'do not do' category for his age grop. We then discussed this norm in light of consequences. What do members of a group do when one person does not recognize the norms and act accordingly? He was able to understand that he was doing something that attracted teasing and that he could make a choice. He could continue to do what he was doing and put up with the teasing, or he could change his behaviour and avoid the teasing. He decided to take a small stuffed animal to school which he could keep with him, perhaps in a pocket, but others would not notice it, and he would try to stop sucking his thumb when in the class-room. Our discussion allowed him to take responsibility for the reaction he was getting from others and make his own decisions about what was important to him.

The foregoing is not meant to suggest that we should condone teasing, or try to make people with autism change to fit in socially in a behaviouristic manner, but rather help them understand the dynamics of social interactions and make their own decisions.

As we move into consideration of relationships, we first estab-lish that how we are as people and how we interact with the world of people consists of emotions and behaviour. We are also address-ing the client as he is at this time in his life. To do this, we have the client place a little dot of clay on the table to represent 'now.' Next we have the client place a sine wave line through the dot and iden-tify it as emotion (which has already been mastered, so no mastery is required at this time). Next, we have the client make a straight line and place it through the now spot, connecting to the ends of the emotion line. This straight line represents *behaviour*, which does need to be mastered. We make sure through the mastery process that the client understands the difference between *emotion* and *behaviour*. We have already, during the mastery of *emotion,* estab-lished that an individual creates his emotions by what he focusses his attention on in the form of thoughts. Emotions and thoughts exist within the *self* as *thoughts* and *feelings.* Behaviour is different because it is action taken in the outside world.

(emotion: self-created energy)

(behaviour: the way one acts or conducts oneself)

As we discuss these concepts, clarifying the difference between emotion and behaviour, we provide examples and elicit examples from the client to illustrate the differences. For example, Kevin, a high school student, was very annoyed about the rule that hats could not be worn in school, and he was behaving in a defiant way and getting into trouble. He found it useful to have his opinion and emotions about that validated and helpful to understand that he was entitled to his thoughts and feelings, but would continue to get into trouble if he acted out his defiance of the rule. He was able to discuss what he wanted in terms of *consequence,* which he had already mastered.

This kind of clarification can be very helpful to anyone and would likely reduce much conflict in the world if more people had the clarity this distinction provides, but it is especially important for individuals with ASD who often have difficulty seeing another's point of view. It can allow them to feel justified in their opinion, while also allowing them to make informed decisions about their behaviour. Kevin decided that he would no longer wear his hat in class because he no longer wanted the negative consequence of his action, even though he still thought it was a silly rule.

The idea that emotion does not necessarily have to be reflected in behaviour is a big idea. Difficulties with anger management and anxiety are often present in autism. Once clients understand that they can choose to separate their actions from their emotions, they seem to be able to control their temper outbursts or meltdowns more effectively.

Relationship

(relationship: interaction of one with another)

In this model, *self* is still standing on the now spot where emotion and behaviour intersect. Added to this is a model of *another*, which stands facing *self*, with an arrow pointing from *self* to the *other*. This represents the idea that self is reaching out and the two people are interacting. The discussion part of this concept involves consideration of different kinds of relationships and interactions with which the client may be familiar. These could include interactions with family members, school-mates, co-workers, friends, and teachers/bosses.

This is a good time to introduce the reciprocal nature of typical social interactions. One of the characteristics of the language usage of individuals with ASD is the tendency to talk at people, but not listen. Sometimes when working with a client who exhibits this tendency, I will ask him to tell me about an activity he has done recently. As he begins to talk, I interrupt him, then ask him to continue, and interrupt him again. Once the pattern is clear, we can discuss how that feels to the person who is talking. Then I talk to the client and have her interrupt me deliberately and notice that I stop talking when I am interrupted, and we can have a good discussion about alternative behaviours when the client wants to say something and *another* is talking.

As an example, I'm going to summarize a case from a book by Tony Attwood called *The Complete Guide to Asperger's Syndrome.* (Attwood 2006)

It is the day of Alicia's birthday party. The doorbell rings and Alicia's mother opens the door to find Jack, the last guest to arrive. The invitation list had been for ten girls and one boy. Alicia's mother had been surprised, thinking that girls her daughter's age usually considered boys to be stupid, but Alicia had said that Jack was different. His family had recently moved into the area and though he had tried, he hadn't made any friends. Alicia thought he was a kind and lonely boy who seemed bewildered by the noise and hectic activity of the playground. He looked cute – a younger Harry Potter, and he knew so much about so many things. Despite the perplexed looks of her friends, she invited him to her party.

Jack was holding a birthday card, with writing strangely illegible for an eight-year-old, and a present, which he immediately gave to Alicia's mother. "You must be Jack," she said. He met this with a blank face. "Yes." She smiled at him, and here I will quote Jack to give you the feeling for his stab at social interaction: "Alicia's birthday present is one of those special dolls that my mum says every girl wants, and she chose it, but what I really wanted to get her was some batteries. Do you like batteries? I do. I have a hundred and ninety-seven batteries. Batteries are really useful. What batteries do you have in your remote controller? I have a special battery from Russia. My dad's an engineer and he was working on an oil pipeline in Russia and he came home with six AAA batteries for me with Russian writing on them. These are my favorite. When I go to bed I like to look at my box of batteries and sort them in alphabetical order before I go to sleep. I always hold one of my Russian batteries as I fall asleep. My mom says I should hug my teddy bear, but I prefer a battery. How many batteries do you have?"

Jack continued to provide a monologue on batteries ... how they are made and what to do with them when the power is exhausted. Alicia's mother felt exhausted too, listening to a lecture that lasted about ten minutes. Despite her subtle signals of needing to be somewhere else, and eventually saying, "I must go and get the party food ready for the party," Jack continued to talk. Alicia's mother noted that it was more like listening to an adult than a child. Jack spoke very eloquently, although he didn't seem to want to listen.

Attwood goes on to describe what happened when Jack went out into the garden, still talking about batteries to the other children. One of the kids tripped him and he fell. Alicia came and gently helped him up. That would be a pretty typical scenario for many children with autism in a social setting.

Another way of helping a client realize the reciprocal nature of relationships is to play board or card games which require taking turns, and then help the client understand that conversations are like taking turns in a game, where both people can have turns talking and listening.

Because the model for *relationship* includes the symbols for *emotion* and *behaviour*, it underscores the idea that the nature of relationships is based on the emotions and behaviours of *self* and *another* or *others*.

The next four concepts relate to how relationships are

established and maintained, and further cement the understanding that there are different kinds of relationships.

(trust: the feeling that another is equal to self)

Trust is a feeling, so the model for this concept is comprised of feeling bubbles attached to the chest of both *self* and *another*. Within each feeling bubble are mini models representing *self* and *another* joined by equal signs. Discussion leads to an understanding that trust is established with one person at a time. Although I may trust the people in my family, that trust is based on the mutual feelings between myself and each person in my family separately. In Derek's case, he might trust his teacher but not share that feeling with the classmates who teased him. We can discuss the 'golden rule' aspect of this concept, thinking about how the client would like to be treated, and that a trusting relationship would mean he would treat other people that way, and would expect the other individual with whom he shared a trust relationship to treat him as the *other* would like to be treated.

(belief: what we feel is actual or real)

As with trust, a relationship based in *belief* is feeling-based and can apply to individual relationships or relationships with groups of people. The model has feeling bubbles attached to the chests of *self* and *another* with a small clay ball in each bubble. The clay ball can represent anything, and indicates a shared feeling of interest or importance. The shared feeling can make establishing a relationship comfortable. People who belong to the same church or religion share moral and spiritual beliefs, and thus find a basis for relationship. People who enjoy camping are likely to find it easy to form relationships with others who share that enjoyment. Discussion can lead to the understanding that friendships are often based on shared enjoyment, or sharing opinions about what is fun or worth doing. Children often make great friends through the sports they play or clubs they belong to. Older clients are often very concerned about their lack of friends, and this concept can open doors for them as they understand that one way to form a friendship is to find an interest and seek out others who share that interest.

An important aspect of this concept is the understanding that one's opinion, or feeling, is valid, as are those of other people. I often have fun comparing likes and dislikes with clients as they come to this understanding. I think lobster is delicious, while the client hates it. Neither is right nor wrong ... just different. My clients are often mystified by the discovery that I have no pets, and do not want to have any pets. We can have a good discussion about how dog-lovers have a lot in common, a passion I do not share. Clients often have things about which they are passionately interested, and it may be difficult for them to understand that not all people share their passion. Discussion can lead to the understanding that they can have good relationships with people who do not share their beliefs, but that shared beliefs can pave the way for good relationships.

(agree: what we think is actual or real)

The first two types of relationships, those based on *trust* and *belief*, are based on feelings within the individual. The next two, *agree* and *rules*, are based on ideas found outside the individual, and help establish and maintain relationships with groups of people and with society in general.

The model for *agree* is similar to that for *belief*, but now the clay balls are in thought bubbles attached to the heads of *self* and *another*, not feeling bubbles attached to the chests. The balls can represent anything the individuals think and agree about. For example, people agree that one cannot take things from a store without paying for the items. In meetings, people agree to how decisions are to be made. My client and I can agree on the fact that a rose is red without sharing the belief that roses are beautiful and smell nice. In other words, we can agree on the known or accepted facts about the rose while disagreeing with our feelings or beliefs about the rose. The Davis definition of *agree* can encompass any sort of agreement. A family may get a dog if the child agrees to walking the dog. A parent may agree to purchase a desired toy if the child agrees to make her bed every day for two weeks. Marital partners may have many agreements about which one does certain tasks within the house. When a family moves, they agree with the new owners or landlord about the moving date. The family has an agreement with the moving company to move their belongings on a certain date. Older clients can appreciate that research is carried out so that people can agree on the facts about the topics researched.

I have found that this is a good time to do some work about arguments. This goes beyond the original intention of Davis for these two concepts of *belief* and *agree,* but it seems to fit, serve a useful purpose, and flow naturally from the concepts.

Many parents report that their children with ASD drive family members crazy with their propensity for arguing. Having difficulty accepting points of view of others is one of the hallmarks of autism, often referred to as lack of having Theory of Mind (Korkmaz 2011). In practical terms, this means that individuals with ASD tend to have a highly egocentric view of the world; they have difficulty understanding that other people may have different thoughts and beliefs than they do. One of the consequences of this kind of thinking is that the individual with ASD will argue unrelentingly for his point of view.

Discussion about the difference between beliefs, opinions, thoughts, or facts can be helpful to loosen this egocentric rigidity of attitude. If we can get to the point where the client can accept that there is no point in arguing about different beliefs, because there is no answer, many arguments can be seen as unnecessary. There is no point in arguing about whether it is fun to have a pet lizard, because some people might hold the belief that it is fun, while others might hold the belief that lizards are boring pets. There is no right or wrong answer. We are halfway there.

Next we can address whether there is any point in arguing about facts, what is thought to be actual or real. If two people are arguing about whether or not lead is safe to eat, they can easily solve the argument by looking it up or going to an expert who knows the answer. Thus, there is really no point in arguing about facts, because the truth can be found to put the matter to rest.

The obvious conclusion is that there is no point in arguing. If we can get to this point, the incessant arguments of many individuals with ASD can be diminished.

(rules: regulations that establish boundaries of acceptable behaviour)

The last basis for relationships we address is *rules.* The model has little arrowheads placed on the behaviour line. These arrow heads mark the boundaries. Within the space between the arrow heads is a small clay tablet or booklet representing 'regulations'. These regulations establish acceptable behaviours.

Discussion can lead clients to the understanding that rules serve a purpose. Many individuals with ASD do not like rules, and are likely to refuse to obey rules they don't like or with which they do not agree. Understanding why rules exist can help soften this attitude. Some rules exist for the safety of people. Examples would be speed limits, driving rules, boating rules, or rules about running around swimming pools. Some rules exist to make things fun; games are nothing more than rule-based activities. Some rules exist for the protection of people or property. Examples would be laws forbidding people to go into someone else's house and take their things, or laws preventing people from attacking other people, or rules about bullying. Some rules exist to make things work better. Examples would be the rule about driving on the right side of the road, or parking between the lines, or taking turns in a gymnastics class.

Once it has been established that rules are useful and serve purposes, we can then have a discussion about the consequences of not following rules: people get hurt; kids won't play with someone who doesn't play by the rules of a game; terrible traffic jams would happen if people didn't drive on the correct side of the road; people can go to jail if they break laws.

It is often a surprise to children to learn that their parents must follow lots of rules. They are accustomed to thinking that only kids have rules to obey, and they yearn for the time when they will be a grown-up and not have to follow rules. They often feel unfairly treated because of the rules they are expected to follow.

As a summary to this segment of the program, we can discuss relationships the client has, and figure out on which of these four concepts the relationships are based. There may be only one, or there may be more than one, in any given relationship. The Davis Autism Approach Program differs from programs that teach specific behaviours or that teach social skills. Our aim is to provide our clients with the understandings they need to be able to observe social behaviour and think about it so they can make informed decisions about how they wish to behave or interact with *others*. We aim to enable them to assess situations and figure out what behaviours are appropriate for that situation.

This brings us to the final segment of the Davis Autism Approach Program. The last four concepts aim to provide clients with the framework that will enable them to make good decisions. There is no attempt within this program to provide a moral code of appropriate rules and regulations that determine what is *good* or *bad*, *right* or *wrong*. Rather, we build on the concepts already mastered such as *consequence, intention, control, responsibility,* and *order*, placing these in the context of behaviours within relationships. This approach allows clients to reach their own decisions within the framework that has been provided to them in their family culture and social norms in the society in which they live.

The models for these concepts continue to include the *emotion* and *behaviour* lines, as well as *self* and *another.* This provides a framework for discussion of the concepts as they affect how one makes choices about what to do and how one makes decisions about how to interact with *others.*

bad
good
wrong
right

Survive, meaning continue as *self,* was mastered earlier. To build on this, we have the client make two mini persons, one standing up and obviously alive, and one lying with eyes closed and arms folded, representing a person not surviving, a person not alive. First, the not alive mini person is placed at one end of the behaviour/emotion lines, and a small arrow is placed between the lines on that side of the model. The client points to that side of the model and says to it, "You represent my emotions and behaviours toward death."

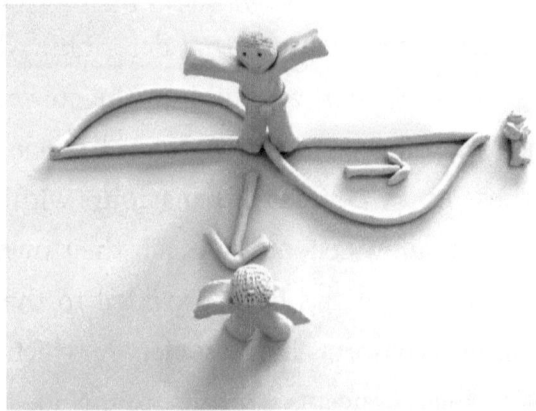

(emotions and behaviour toward death)

The difference between emotion and behaviour has already been established, but this provides a good time to review this idea and make sure that the client is clear about the distinction. Discussion at this point can elicit examples of emotions that would lead toward death, such as anger, fear, hatred, or anxiety. Some clients will leave it that simply, while others may be interested in why or how negative emotions, what we call stress or distress, can lead to physiological reactions that are harmful to *self* and would contribute to poor health and eventually death. Similarly, we can discuss behaviours that would be harmful to *self*, such as running into oncoming traffic, eating a poor diet, refusing to take medicine to treat an infection, or not brushing one's teeth.

Next the client places the alive mini person at the other end of the emotion/behaviour lines, and a small arrow between the lines.

The client points to that side of the model and says to it, "You represent my emotions and behaviours toward life."

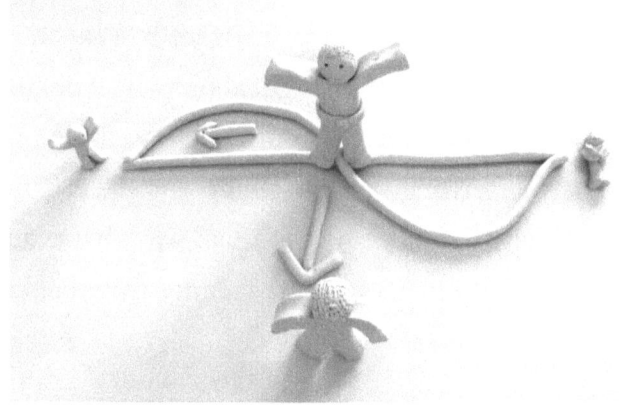

(emotions and behaviour toward life)

Discussion can elicit the idea that positive emotions such as love, happiness, and calmness lead to better physical health, and, therefore, toward life. Behaviours such as eating a good diet, getting enough sleep, brushing teeth, and getting exercise lead to good health and, therefore, to life.

(bad: emotions and behaviours that do not support survival)

In this model, there is a dominant arrow pointing to the side of the model representing toward death. Discussion of this concept can lead the client to think about what would constitute *bad* emotions in himself, and how he could instigate bad (negative) emotions in *others*. It can also lead to insight about what constitutes bad behaviour toward *self* or *others*. This provides another opportunity for discussion concerning the possibility of feeling negatively toward *another* without behaving in a bad way that would harm her, reinforcing the ability to separate feelings from behaviour.

(good: emotions and behaviours that support survival)

In this model, there is a dominant arrow pointing to the side of the model representing toward life. Discussion of this concept provides the opposite of the discussion about *bad*, allowing the client to think about what would constitute *good* emotions and behaviour in *self* and *others*. It can also lead to a discussion about the potential role of *self* in fostering life in *self* and *others*.

(wrong: actions not in support of survival)

In this model, the dominant arrow is pointing to the behaviour line on the death side of the model. While the concept of *bad* refers to both *emotions* and *behaviour*, wrong refers only to *behaviour*. This provides an opportunity to reinforce the idea that no feelings or emotions are wrong. They just are. This is an important point to validate the feelings of clients. It can be helpful for them to realize that, although negative emotions may be harmful to themselves and therefore labelled as *bad*, they are not *wrong*. It can also provide another opportunity for clients to understand the difference between emotions and behaviour, and that while no emotions are *wrong*, behaviours can be.

(right: action that supports survival)

In this model, the dominant arrow moves to the life side of the model pointing to the behaviour line. As with the *wrong* concept, this provides further opportunity to explore the difference between emotions and behaviour. As these distinctions become meaningful to the client, he is in a better position to make the choices that will lead to his desired outcomes. It is assumed that most clients would prefer to position themselves on the *good* and *right* side in a given situation, and these concepts give them the means to make decisions that will place them where they want to be.

Now What?

Mastery of the Social Integration concepts does not include exploration of the environment. These concepts must be integrated into the client's daily interactions with others in his life. The completion of the program marks a sort of graduation. It represents a milestone in the client's life, but as with any graduation, it marks the beginning of the next chapter. Now it is up to the client to experience life through the new lens of the concepts he has mastered.

In family dynamics, when one member of the family changes, others in the family also must change to fit the new relationship paradigm. When one individual completes a Davis concept-based program, changes in behaviour are expected and will require changes in the other family members. Some parents adjust to the changes in their loved one easily, and others seek assistance in learning how to change their parenting style to maximize the positive changes in their loved one and foster continued development.

One thing that can happen as clients develop a stronger sense of *self* is a display of developing autonomy. This can be similar to the developmental stage of young children we refer to as the 'terrible twos'. In typically developing children, that happens at around the age of two. In individuals with ASD, it can happen when they individuate, so families sometimes have to endure that stage, even in teenagers. Fortunately, the passage through this stage for our clients doesn't usually take nearly as long as it does for two-year-olds, but it can be trying. Handling this growing sense of autonomy as one would lovingly handle a two-year-old having a tantrum is the best way to reinforce the concepts and allow the individual with ASD to integrate the concepts into his life.

From this point on, the individual moves through her life, growing and changing as we all do through our experiences. The next part of the book provides insight into how this process has taken place with several clients.

Thank you for taking this journey with me. I hope it has given you some new ways to think about autism and the treatment of individuals with ASD. All of us who have the gift of using these methods are most grateful to Ronald D. Davis for his insight and inspiration, and for his taking responsibility to bring his ideas to the world in such a useful manner.

PART FOUR
Putting It All Together

a. Veronica's Story

The day Veronica and I began the Social Integration part of the program, Veronica and her mother stopped at a shopping plaza on the way home. A young man went up to their truck to try to sell them some candles. Veronica talked with him, answering many questions about herself, and bought some things from him. When they drove away, she told her mother he was nice, good looking, and she expected to be thinking about him a lot in the future. Veronica's mother was cracking up inside, trying not to let Veronica see. Veronica had been a man-hater as far back as her mother could remember and not the least interested in boys or in talking to anyone except her mother. She had dropped out of school and had been living as a recluse in her mother's basement for a couple of years. When they arrived home that day, Veronica suggested that they might go for a walk, even though it was very cold outside. Her mother readily agreed, as Veronica was never willing to do anything physical. They went for a walk.

Six months after her program finished, Veronica was taking sewing lessons, able to sit outside and even nap in the hammock, and go to malls. She had been having panic attacks regularly before her program, but had not had one in the six months since her program.

....

b. Matthew's Story

My name is Cathy, and I am the mother of a wonderful son whose name is Matthew. When Matthew was eight years old, I wrote a letter describing his disabilities and the effects they were having on his life and ours. What follows is an excerpt from that letter:

> The impairment stemming from Matthew's disorders has, in one manner or another, infiltrated every aspect of his life. He is unable to wash and dress himself without assistance. He is unable to sustain peer relationships. He is unable to respond in an appropriate manner to social stimuli, which has led to violent physical and/or emotional outbursts. He is unable to go anywhere unaccompanied. He has extensive difficulties in adapting to a school environment. Since Matthew's impairment affects him 100% of the time, attending to Matthew's many and varying needs is required on our part 100% of the time.
>
> Matthew was born with the conditions of Autism and ADHD, which manifested themselves very early on, as evidenced by his delay in reaching physical and

cognitive developmental milestones such as talking, walking, and socializing.

From the time he was very little, Matthew seemed to live in his own world, disconnected from everyone and everything around him. It took a lot to get him out of that world and into our present life. If anyone tried to abruptly make Matthew change his state of mind, he reacted swiftly and violently, screaming and having a full-blown meltdown. The disconnectedness and language delay became so pronounced that before he reached two years of age, we took Matthew to an audiologist and otolaryngologist to have his hearing checked. Everything checked out perfectly normal. However, at home, Matthew's behaviour and interests remained far behind what was age appropriate. His fear of social situations, not only with adults but also with peers who were strangers, prompted me to begin "\'mother and child' preschool classes with him. It took most of the first year for Matthew to even begin showing an interest in activities, and only with my direct assistance. Matthew did not participate in group play or group socializing games and songs. As Matthew began his school career, we became used to being called to the dismissal door to have what became a daily conference with his teacher. Each day, Matthew did something to get into trouble. This trouble was always linked to defiance of established rules, socially inappropriate behaviour, or physically bothering another child in class. In desperation for an answer, we had Matthew tested for ADHD at the end of his grade one academic year. He more than qualified for having ADHD.

In fact, once he had that first diagnosis, we began our search for an answer to help our son. We tried drug therapies—with decidedly negative results. We had not been enthusiastic about the concept of drugs in the first place, but desperation can lead you down many paths you never thought you would follow! In fairly short order, we stopped the medication and resolved to continue our search for an answer for Matthew. It came in October of 2012—six months after Matthew's initial diagnosis of ADHD. My sister had seen a feature about the Davis Dyslexia Program on *Global News* at 6:00 p.m. She called me immediately after seeing the interview and told me that this sounded like something I should investigate. Even though Matthew had not been diagnosed with dyslexia, she felt convinced that I must watch the episode online and find out if and how this program could help Matthew. So I did. I Googled the keywords "Davis Dyslexia" and found a Davis facilitator online. I called the next day, and within a month, Matthew started the Davis program for dyslexia—yes! He was dyslexic, along with having ADHD! (Although these diagnoses answered many questions for us, we experienced a great frustration over the lost years where Matthew remained undiagnosed.) By lunch-time of the first day, his facilitator called me into the office and we discussed her observations of the morning with him. She said that Matthew actually fit the criteria—overwhelmingly so—for autism, specifically Asperger's syndrome! Do you know what I felt at that moment?

Nothing but relief.

Here, at last, was an answer—and it all made so much sense! Ah, hindsight! I willingly and enthusiastically gave her permission to follow the autism program facilitation. The results were incredible, and changes began immediately.

Matthew's life in those early years, prior to his proper diagnosis of autism and his participation in the Davis program, was full of challenges, large and small, but it was the daily struggles that wore everyone down over the long term.

> Matthew is unable to independently wash and dress himself. The 'simple' act of brushing his teeth would regularly take a minimum of twenty minutes if left to his own devices, with little to no progress by the end, and always ended up with us having to complete the brushing for him.

> Matthew has an extremely diminished lack of awareness of his environment and himself in it. This, in turn, leads him to do things that many regard as socially unacceptable for a boy his age. Whether it is humming when he is bored, or loudly stating his displeasure in being forced to participate in a given activity—a meal, school lesson, or even a movie—it has resulted in Matthew being publicly chastised, even by strangers.

> However, while Matthew has a low level of personal awareness, he has a high level of awareness of, and

intolerance for, many outside stimuli. Television shows, singing, being asked to complete a task—there is often little warning of his explosive reactions. As a result, we must always be aware of what is going on in Matthew's vicinity, so as to avoid or manage potentially explosive situations between him and those around him, which can arise from what most people would consider the most mundane of activities.

As a result of his social missteps, Matthew is constantly corrected and chastised, not only by us, his parents, but also by those who have a duty of care for him—teachers, especially. The constant correction causes him to become visibly frustrated and stressed. We have observed that Matthew's tics, idiosyncratic behaviours, and stims increase as his frustration and stress levels increase. These tics, stims, and behaviours further set him apart from his 'normal' peers and further isolate him

Matthew's inability to predictably behave in a socially acceptable manner has also made it impossible for our family to go out for meals in any social setting that does not involve family. Even when there is extended family present, the level of tension that we experience is so high that these events are merely tolerated for the sake of family ties, and not because we get any social enjoyment from them.

Matthew's impairment has had a strong negative effect on his ability to learn and be educated. We have tried every avenue available for his educational success—private, public, and finally, homeschooling. In his first (private) school, we thought that the smaller class sizes and lower teacher to student ratio would benefit him. However, after four years of continuous complaints about his behaviour and inability to socialize appropriately, we moved him to the public system, where the increased access to resources would allow him to integrate better in school. Unfortunately, this was not the case. No greater number of resources could cancel out Matthew's inability to accept social norms, or increase his attentiveness in class. At the end of his first year in public school, it was suggested that Matthew was unable to handle the full school day, and that he should be attending only half days in-class. The other half of the day, he would work with me at home. This, ultimately, led to our decision to homeschool him full-time.

I must note that underlying all Matthew's issues was a fundamental physical weakness caused by lack of sleep. This was, perhaps, the most frustrating and debilitating to all of us, because it sapped all of our strength. We tried everything we could to correct this situation, but just could not succeed.

At bedtime, Matthew requires either me or my husband to sit with him in his room until he falls asleep, which never takes less than forty-five minutes and often stretches longer—from one to three hours, in the worst case. We have tried everything—early and late bedtimes, bathing before bed, snack and no snack, stories and no stories, music, white noise, a prescribed bedtime routine and a more relaxed approach, incentives, even consequences for not going to sleep ... as if he actually was doing this on purpose! We have given everything its due time to work, but the truth is that he simply cannot fall asleep without great struggle, every night, regardless of how tired he is. He often apologizes to us, telling us that he is trying to fall asleep, but he just can't. He is so remorseful, it breaks my heart to hear him apologize for something he cannot help.

While one of us sits with Matthew to help him sleep, the other parent puts our youngest son to bed. Unfortunately, the responsibility of putting our younger daughter to sleep often falls on our eldest child, Mary Elizabeth.

If the evening ended when the children were all put to bed, late as it is, that would at least put an endpoint on the day. However, Matthew does not sleep through the night. He regularly wakes up, several times in the night, every night. When he wakes up, he calls out loudly to my husband or me, rather than just coming quietly to our room, because he is scared to walk in the darkened hallways (yes, even with nightlights). The loud calling risks waking the other children, so we take turns hopping out of bed at the first sound of his voice and rush to his bedside to calm him and sit with him, once again, until he falls back to sleep. The vicious cycle of sleeplessness is breaking us down, both physically and in spirit. It seems that there is no hope!

This was our life for over seven years—endless cycles of sleeplessness, broken sleep patterns, and a gradual erosion of hope that it would ever end.

The Davis program changed everything. Imagine a family—two parents and four young children—hanging desperately on to the bottom end of a frayed rope. That was our family—at the end of our rope, and feeling as though we were going to plunge into a dark abyss of hopelessness. Until we found Davis.

At the time, Matthew was one of the youngest people to ever have gone through the program. Because of his brilliant mind, and likely a bit because of my obvious desperation, the facilitator took a chance on us. Once Matthew went through the Davis Autism Program, we began to see little changes right away. We held our expectations in check—that he would continue to behave more reasonably, to respect others, to be present in the world and with the people around him, to respond to unexpected situations calmly. Would this program—could it—help our autistic son understand how to behave in our 'normal' world? Incredibly, we found progressive success over the months and even years that followed the program. Matthew will always be autistic; indeed, autism is part of what makes him the kind-hearted, loving, brilliant genius and wonderful person that he is! I would not want him to be other than who he is today. But if we had not found Davis, I know, without any doubts, that he, and we, would not be here today. The support we received throughout the years has made us consider Matthew's facilitator a special member of our extended family!

We want to help other families and children suffering from the hell that lack of adequate information is causing in their lives. If we could give every person on the spectrum a chance to experience the Davis program, we would. The Davis program gave us back our life—a life we thought we had lost and would never have again. Today, Matthew is a socialized, intelligent young man, who accepts responsibility for his actions and has integrated into the social fabric of society very well. And for that, we thank Ron Davis and Matthew's facilitator, Beth. Alone, before the Davis program, our lives were characterized by emotional pain, frustration, and often hopelessness. Together with Davis, we are a happy, well-adjusted family, and Matthew has a bright, successful future ahead of him!

···

c. Liam's Story

Our son, Liam, was diagnosed with Asperger's when he was eight years old, and he faced many challenges. The diagnosis was daunting, but the pursuit of getting the support and tools for him to be successful was also a rocky road to navigate. Not all kids on the spectrum are the same, and finding the right fit of therapies and support was a guessing game. We were cautious about the Davis approach at first, but Liam's approach and acceptance of the program came quickly. The mother/son team, Cathy and Desmond, had an instant impact on Liam. His words: "They get me." That is the single most important attribute for Liam from a trust and measurement of success perspective.

Liam's challenges included over-reactions (very little emotional control), change (transition from one task to another), lack of cause and effect (acted spontaneously), self-loathing (especially when a mistake was made), anxiety around completing tasks, or feeling overloaded with tasks to list a few.

The Davis program resonated with Liam predominately through the clay model building, which acted as an implant into his brain. For a visual learner, this technique really has an impact. But, of course, the facilitators', Cathy's and Desmond's, profound understanding of Liam propelled him to success. They worked to provide Liam with solutions from real life examples and in real time. We saw an improvement very quickly. He still required prompting to cue him when to use his tools, but once prompted, he would easily execute them on his own.

Liam still gets frustrated, but he knows how to mitigate his reaction and control any escalation. He has more self-control to keep himself grounded and aligned. He understands cause and effect and works very hard proactively to plan ahead to offset any situation that he now knows will, or could, set him off.

We are so thankful to have found Cathy and her Davis program clinic, and are profoundly grateful for the help it's given to our Liam.

....

d. Meryle's Story

The Davis program changed me in ways that made me able to control and regulate my Asperger's symptoms, rather than having my symptoms control me. I don't have panics attacks anymore, and I don't spiral into meltdowns anymore. I now recognize when my mind and body are going into an episode and can take action to calm myself before the episode starts. It's incredibly empowering to be able to recognize the early warning signs in myself and do something proactive about it. I can even self-stim (usually repeated leg flank rubbing) and know that I won't trigger a meltdown in myself from being "too autistic." I am able to form better, less abusive relationships because I learned about proper interpersonal relationships skills that helped me identify when I was being taken advantage of.

Things like the concept of time changed drastically for me. After treatment, I started being able to arrive on time for things and even got better at communicating when I realized I was going to be late. My fights with family members stopped because I was better able to express my boundaries in a way that got me listened to, and my feelings acknowledged. I started being able to describe the feelings in my body and identifying them as they are. I now know what is me and what isn't me, and I no longer confuse other people's feelings for my own. This new ability to feel my own feelings helped me recognize that I had food allergies, because I was finally able to notice that my stomach hurt all the time. Once I started cutting out foods I was allergic to, I lost a lot of anxiety, became a lot calmer, and thought and spoke clearer. I was even able to cut back on my self-injurious habits, because I realized the pain I used to inflict on myself was a coping mechanism to distract from the pain my body felt from always having allergic reactions to what I was eating daily. I was able to figure this out and save my health because of what I learned in my Davis program.

Let me say this specifically about Cathy Dodge Smith: She is a saint and a miracle worker. She is the most patient and non-judgemental person I have worked with. She is the ideal Davis facilitator, and I hope that anyone taking this program gets to work with a facilitator as wonderful, understanding, and skilled in dealing with autistic people as Cathy is.

Cathy and this program changed my entire life. I used to shut down emotionally and be non-verbal, and now I work as a voice actor, writer, and singer. I've even learned to turn my vocal tics and fidgeting into sound and rhythm instigators for song and poetry writing.

After the Davis program, I took Second City improv courses, and although it was very uncomfortable at times, I was able to learn strong eye contact and listening skills, which are both key to performing improv, in ways that I would not have been able to do without taking the Davis Approach first. I feel like I have gained access to all the fun, creative, positive, and different abilities my Asperger's mind has while being able to bypass and easily control the parts of my Asperger's that used to hurt me. The Davis Autism Approach saves lives, and I believe Ron Davis has brought a powerful gift to the world.

....

e. Luke's Story

All of the preceding stories described individuals with ASD who were highly verbal from the beginning of their Davis journey. Luke's story describes the journey of a six-year-old boy who was completely non-verbal when he began to work with Desmond. What follows is an account of what happens before a Davis program while the child is becoming oriented, in this case assisted by a NOIT (see p. 14), and ready for a more formal program. Luke's mother, Lisa, kept detailed notes, and the story is told in her own words (though the names and identifying information have been changed). As you will become aware, they travelled from their home to work with Desmond and were staying in a hotel.

Though a seemingly healthy baby, from the age of two Luke started to regress developmentally each day, and quickly lost the limited speech ability he had gained as a toddler. He appeared to start shutting down into his own world. It was like his body and brain were no longer linked.

We tried everything we could think of or find, but nothing seemed to help until the Davis methods. At their first meeting, Luke took to Desmond like a duck to water. He greeted Desmond with a huge smile and then a wonderful hug within one minute, unusual behavior for Luke. It was AMAZING to see their connection. Luke knows he's the man to help, You should see the way Desmond communicates with Luke – they exchange the most wonderful eye contact and I almost feel an intruder of their space.

Desmond discovered that Luke loves horses, so he had arranged with a local farmer to take Luke to her farm to visit the horses while introducing Luke to the NOIT. We followed Desmond to the horses and fitted Luke with his NOIT. IMMEDIATE positive response. Luke seemed aware and in control of all of his actions. His eyes went really wide as though seeing the world in a new way. Desmond said 'shall we go and water the plants in my garden Luke?' Immediately Luke took Desmond to his car and pulled his hand to the passenger door, so Luke went in the car with Desmond and I followed them – I had been officially dumped – a great sign! Desmond and Luke just 'pottered' in the garden – Luke never potters! But then all of a sudden, around 30 minutes later Luke ran off (old behaviours returned and he was agitated). So after 20 minutess we agreed we'd go back to the offices. This is the magical bit....As I put Luke in the car Desmond asked me "Can you hear the NOIT, Lisa?' and I couldn't! Desmond replied 'It's fallen off, I'll go and find it!" The NOIT was right at the spot where Luke's behaviours had changed from being oriented to non–oriented. It was clear evidence that a visible and noticeable change in Luke's behavior took place when he lost the NOIT.

On day two, I left Luke on his own with Desmond. When I returned to pick him up, I was astounded to find him calm, and clearly listening to everything Desmond said. day three was a day off, so I took Luke to the Toronto Aquarium. We arrived at the train station and Luke was sitting calmly when all of a sudden he became very agitated. I realized the NOIT had stopped working because I hadn't switched it with the fully charged one! So, we drove back to the hotel (missed our train) and collected the fully charged NOIT. Immediately Luke regained orientation and was calm again. We returned to the train station and Luke and I sat on the bench having a hug while waiting for the train. This is the magical bit......Luke gave a long sigh, then rested his head on my shoulder and said 'Mum' as clear as anything! I could not believe it, I was so shocked I didn't know how to feel, but I did feel an overwhelming sense of tension leave my shoulders.

We got on the train and enjoyed a peaceful journey. Luke sat on my knees the whole way and just took in everything. To witness him so aware of his surroundings is wonderful. I am so proud of how Luke is taking this new world in his stride. At times I think I've struggled more than Luke to take all of the new information in. When we arrived in Toronto we walked through the station and although Luke gently held my hand at times, he walked independently for most of the 10-minute walk. He only flapped his arms a few times and didn't run off once! I was able to relax, which was all very surreal for me – we are always on a high state of alert when with Luke to ensure we keep him safe 24/7 – it's been exhausting! For the first time I could enjoy taking in the new scenery around me.

We arrived at the aquarium, which was incredible, but I noticed Luke becoming agitated in a controlled way due to the noise and crowds. This proved to me Luke was incredibly aware of his environment as previously crowds and noise have never bothered him simply because he was in his own world and unaware. Another positive. I allow him to just stay close and reassure him that "It's all ok," while he readjusts to this new world he's experiencing. This is a reason why our daytrips and afternoons out are important to this whole healing process. We need to show Luke he can cope with everything, and that he's safe. To enable us to do those two things we have to expose him to different situations – slowly but surely.

Luke was intrigued by the fish and would study them as they swam past. At one point we found a tunnel we could crawl through so off we went. Luke was so engaged in this, he lined up patiently, copied the other children and crouched down onto his hands and knees and crawled through. He very rarely copies others and his observational skills were fantastic.

We then walked to have a spot of lunch and at 2:00 p.m. travelled home. Luke was walking brilliantly the whole time but then all of a sudden he ran off. Thankfully he returned swiftly and we continued our walk back to the train station. After approximately a one-minute walk Luke was agitated again and something made me check that his NOIT was still in place. It had fallen off! I was slightly panicked as it could be anywhere. However, I realized it may possibly have fallen off at the spot where he ran off, so we marched back and there was the NOIT lying on the ground at the exact spot. Once I stopped panicking about losing the NOIT I contemplated what a great piece of evidence this was that the NOIT is making a difference to Luke. When it falls off it is like a switch goes off in Luke and he immediately reverts back to his old ways. Incredible.

This afternoon we relaxed, went for a cool swim, and then watched a movie in the Movie room here at the hotel. This was another first. Luke sat independently next to me and watched the movie for at least 45 minutes without moving! His breathing was calm and regular and he was very content. I didn't know what to do with myself and felt a spare part but I soon reveled in this new experience. Luke then came and sat on me and we hugged. I still cannot get over how Luke's hyper-activity and fidgeting disappear when he is wearing the NOIT. It is remarkable and the transformation is amazing!

Sleep has always been elusive for Luke, and therefore for my husband and me, as we would take turns trying to get some sleep. After Luke's forth day with Desmond, he slept from 7:00 p.m. until 5:00 a.m., which was amazing. When we arrived at Desmond's office in the morning, Luke just wanted hugs with Desmond. So Desmond ran with this.

They hugged for over two hours – Luke barely moved! During this time Desmond did loads of breathing techniques with Luke to help his body and brain link and made repetitive sounds in Luke's ear. I watched Luke just sink into Desmond. His body was so still and calm; I have never seen him at such peace!

I was lucky enough to spend two hours with Desmond's mum who was just as inspiring and had me hanging off her every word. She told me her story and I could have listened to her for hours. She really understood me, my position and how damn hard it has been with Luke; yet she had this air of positivity about her that helped my hope grow even more. I asked her for her top tip and she said "You take each day as it comes and just love Luke!"

I then observed Luke imitate Desmond's sounds. This was amazing as Luke does make sounds but not in response to someone else's and certainly not the same sound as the person made. He's been really, really peaceful all day and even fell asleep in the car this afternoon (paying for it now, though, as he's still awake and showing no signs of going to sleep). After dinner he was adamant he wanted to go in the movie room so I allowed him to take me in there and for a whole hour he sat on me so very still He didn't move once and his breathing was nice and consistent. It was completely alien to me to be that still for so long with Luke; it was lovely. He was also aware of the other children in the room and would gently turn his head when one of them moved.

This was a great example of Luke being oriented and therefore aware of his surroundings and absolutely fine with it.

While in the car on our way home I had heard Luke repeat the sound he and Desmond had been making earlier. I followed Desmond's advice and copied the sound and then Luke repeated it again on cue about three times! He then gave me a big smile when I said "Good talking, Luke." It was as if he knew what he was doing. He's been repeating the sound while lying in bed, too – great, great news. Desmond said he wanted sounds today and he got it!

Just as I didn't think anything could match yesterday's experiences, it did.

Luke slept from 7:15 p.m. to 5:00 a.m. again, which is great for him. He is certainly much more peaceful when asleep now and barely moves. He wakes up a bit groggy so I still think he could do with a little more, but it's better than it's been in a long while. My husband and I might start to feel a little more 'normal' if this sleep pattern continues.

Luke did not want to sit and eat breakfast this morning; he just wanted to go to the garage. I'm convinced he just wanted to get to Desmond. We arrived at 9:00 a.m. and Luke took himself straight off to the toilet independently and then returned to Desmond and promptly led him to his chair and settled down for their morning hug. Desmond immediately started his breathing techniques with Luke and I watched Luke just melt into Desmond.

Desmond and I were able to spend a few minutes to catch up on where Luke is in relation to the Davis Method and Luke is following the steps in the right order at rapid speed – he's so receptive to it, it's incredible! Luke had a new energy about him today; he was really excited as though he was ready for that next leap of faith. Desmond constantly tells Luke "You're awesome Buddy", "I'm so pleased to see you today", "You're so smart Luke", and "Thank you," for every single positive action. A tremendous amount of respect passes between Luke and Desmond.

We also spoke about the night Luke didn't fall asleep until 10:00 p.m. despite looking really tired at 7:00 p.m. Desmond asked me whether I had taken the NOIT *off and then put him straight to bed...I had! For the first time since we arrived I ignored our bedtime routine of bath with Epsom salts (highly recommend this for any child as it really does calm them), supper, a bit of* TV *and cuddles an hour before bedtime. This was a mistake. This meant Luke's brain immediately reverted back to being out of control again and back in the 'fog'. Consequently, he became wired and hyperactive. I had forgotten how Luke used to be like this 24/7. Although it was a bit fraught at the time it's another piece of terrific evidence the* NOIT *works effectively.*

Luke has not wet himself in the five days he's been with Desmond – amazing! On our first day here, Luke had wet every single pair of underwear and shorts that I had packed. When Desmond took Luke to the park today, Luke waited his turn for the slide with the other children. He didn't push in and instead respected their personal space. Another first! Luke then slid purposefully down the slide towards Desmond with his arms stretched outwards four times in a row. Luke was signaling to Desmond he was ready with great eye contact at the top of the slide – Luke was 'playing' with Desmond – an amazing sign he was present and oriented. Before today Luke had never initiated play with anyone.

Also Luke has stopped putting everything into his mouth which means his other senses (sight, hearing, touch and smell) are beginning to kick in and Desmond summed this point up really clearly for me. A toddler will place objects in his/her mouth to find out whether they like or dislike something as their gut never lies. Desmond explained that Luke's eyes and ears have been lying to him all of the time because what they are relaying back to Luke's brain is not what he has been hearing or seeing in his mind! Taste is the only sense he has been able to trust as to whether he likes/dislikes something. Today they went to the grocery store to buy some strawberries and Desmond encouraged Luke to smell the limes, lemons and grapefruits to awaken his sense of smell and help him to trust it again. Makes perfect sense once it's explained so well.

I cannot get over how I need to give Luke space to walk on his own, dress himself, feed himself (although he would still much rather eat with his fingers) and generally embrace being independent. I need to start forcing myself to step back and give him that freedom, but it really is a new feeling. I need to shift it quicker so I don't block any potential progress. Luke also sighed independently three times in the car on our way to the Mall. This is great as he's self-regulating using 'release', which is critical to being fully oriented.

This afternoon we visited a shopping mall and Luke liked being in the big open space, but hated being in a store so we didn't last too long. We then watched Shrek 3 from 5:00 to 6:00 p.m. Again Luke was still and sat on his own chair very content! I felt I could really relax again and just enjoy siting peacefully next to him. I honestly have to pause during these moments and reflect on what a new way of being this is for us.

Overall, another brilliant day! Tomorrow we are going to Desmond's house and meeting Beth Shier, who is the head of NOIT *Research, for* lunch so I am looking forward to seeing how Luke adjusts to that situation – something tells me he's going to love it.

Luke was not his usual calm self this morning following his bath and the attachment of his NOIT. He wasn't too bad but there was a slight edge to him that I couldn't remove despite many words of encouragement and praise. I couldn't put my finger on what was wrong, but I knew it was different from the Luke I have witnessed this week. He seemed slightly agitated by his own skin again. However, he was still following instructions, taking in some of his surroundings and aware of some of his actions. He just didn't seem to have the clarity he's demonstrated throughout the week and appeared unsettled. We visited the grocery store and purchased a plant for Desmond for his garden to say thank you for an amazing first week. Luke pushed the cart really well and negotiated the people walking towards him, although he clearly decided the row of canned peanuts could take a hit. They made a great sound as they clanged to the floor! He was also able to pick up the juice and throw it (literally) into the cart upon my requests. He was in control and seemed happy to comply with my instructions. I just couldn't shake off the feeling that it was still different.

When we arrived at Desmond's house we met his wonderful wife, Joanne, his step-daughter Alanna and her handsome son Aiden, his dad Ron, and Dr. Cathy, as well as Beth Shier. Desmond and Joanne's home was so calm that I instantly felt relaxed. I immediately told Desmond that something seemed different today. Desmond could feel it too, and Luke didn't embrace Desmond in his normal way. He struggled to focus but it was still an improvement from when we've visited friends' houses in the past when we wouldn't be able to sit down because Luke would require constant watching as he paced people's homes.

Desmond took Luke upstairs to meet his dog. Suddenly Des called from the stairwell, "I think I know what's wrong and why Luke is different. There is a crackle in the ting sound" Beth immediately jumped up and went to check the NOIT. She gave it a clean and asked Desmond to observe Luke for a further minute to see if that was the problem.

We sat down to brunch and then the chaos from our past returned. Luke was like a wild animal, unable to sit on his bottom, grabbing and squashing fistfuls of berries, grabbing my hair and climbing over me as well as leaving a trail of destruction on the table. The table and I looked a mess and my anxiety level rocketed! Thankfully, Desmond came to my rescue and whisked Luke back upstairs and calmed him down through the use of his breathing activities. I was in a house I had never visited before, I should have felt embarrassed and mortified at the state of both myself and the table; however, I was surrounded by a small group of wonderful individuals who just 'got it.'

Dr. Cathy and I had spoken earlier this week about the judgements of others that parents of children who are 'different' have to endure day after day. My husband and I have experienced this countless times. It's heartbreaking and disempowering, because we have learned that no matter how many times we try to explain that Luke really does not mean to do this, they just don't 'get it', and the judgement hits our core (and my heart) every single time. That day, instead of judging, everyone sat round the table trying to work out what was going on. They knew something was impacting Luke's neurological function. I felt humbled by their actions and words of wisdom – imagine if everyone thought in this way. Beth investigated the NOIT further and she found one of the wires had come loose. The sense of relief I felt was immense and yet again we had further evidence of the positive impact the NOIT was having on Luke. So, it was all systems go. Within a few moments our bags were packed, we said our goodbyes and drove straight to the Oakville Success Centre to collect a new NOIT. Within minutes Luke's whole body relaxed and calm returned...phew!

As we drove home I reflected on this experience and realized Luke was unhappy being back in that chaotic world, and as Desmond said, "Luke wanted it to stop!" This is remarkable when you consider a week ago that foggy/chaotic world was Luke's safe place, where he would escape when he didn't want to comply or acknowledge us. Now, through his behaviour he was telling us to make it stop. He IS now ready. A slightly traumatic hour or so has given me so much more belief that we are on the right path, so onwards and upwards.

I enjoyed the most enlightening conversation with Beth and Dr. Cathy who explained the NOIT'S origins. Beth and I also spoke about how Ron Davis is constantly updating the NOITs to be even more efficient, So we returned to our hotel, covered in berries and slightly worn out, but thankfully Luke retained his calmness and fell asleep peacefully at 7:00 p.m.

Here's to a good night's sleep and a great day tomorrow!

Week Two: **Resistance Day**

Today started abruptly at 1:00 a.m. Luke crawled into my bed and was restless until 4.30 a.m. when he finally fell asleep. This was the second morning in a row that he had followed this pattern, and although he frequently wakes in the night, now he seemed to want constant reassurance with a hug. I happily obliged and told him it was all OK but that he really did need to go to sleep. We woke up in a thick haze at *approximately 7.30 a.m. and following a strong coffee for myself we got ready for the day.*

Luke was not as calm as he's been. Immediately I worried the NOIT *wasn't working fully following yesterday's unsettled behavior, but it seemed to be* OK. *We arrived at Desmond's for 9:00 a.m. and I explained that Luke was acting a bit 'odd' and a little unsettled. Desmond checked the* NOIT *and confirmed all was fine and that the tinging sound was perfect. I said my goodbyes and left Luke in the very capable hands of Desmond. Following my verbal goodbye, Luke gently yet purposefully grabbed my hand, pulled it to his chest and then pushed it away. Desmond very quickly spotted this and said, "He's just said goodbye, Lisa", so I left them in peace.*

As I left I couldn't shrug the feeling of "Is this the resistance day I've been waiting for since we arrived." You see, Luke is the master of resistance and this is at the point many of the professionals who have worked with Luke in the past have walked away, leaving us with no answers. I have watched Luke do this time and time again. I know that many children test adults like this to see if they will stick by them, and Luke is the true master of testing adults, and not many pass his test. I dread it when it comes around because I know I have to begin a new research path to find help for Luke.

Part of me applauds Luke for this – why should he let anyone into his world if they do not truly believe in what they are doing or even more importantly be prepared to push their own boundaries in terms of their professional knowledge and methods? I know Luke has been searching for the very best and no-one else will do. We have witnessed Luke refuse to comply with diagnostic tests on purpose and completely manipulate a scenario that manifests itself into a situation that leaves the professionals aghast. Only the very best (and brave) have been able to see this with their own eyes and not deem him as 'unaware of his actions.' Ironically, Luke has been incredibly aware and in control of his actions in those scenarios.

So, it was 'Resistance Day' for Desmond and I was very aware of the importance of Desmond conquering today – and conquer it he did. Desmond called me tonight and explained how he had showed Luke he's here to stay and no matter what Luke put in front of him, Desmond wasn't budging. Through the positive Davis Autism Approach, Desmond continued with his breathing techniques intensely for approximately 55 minutes while Luke pulled all of his tricks out of the bag. He stood on the chairs, climbed over Desmond, didn't fully respond to instructions (despite hearing them), increased his hyperactivity and flapping of his arms; the list goes on....

Luke was also starving, despite having had a big breakfast, and this just made resistance day even tougher because Luke does not like the feeling of hunger and will repetitively hunt for food and will not settle until his hunger disappears. Desmond explained that most importantly he 'requested' Luke to behave in a certain way that empowered Luke and then when Luke responded positively Desmond gave him a tight hug and said, "Thank you so much, Luke." So although Luke was misbehaving, he was empowered to make the right choice which was then rewarded with positive recognition of the behaviour.

This all makes perfect sense and is very logical once explained, but here's the bit that is the unique part. Desmond explained he made sure his energy level was low from the moment Luke entered his room. We have all experienced that party, meeting, or interview when we walk into a room and we either feel happy or sad, excited or nervous, at ease or uncomfortable, or simply just not right. This is because we unconsciously pick up on people's thought processes and subsequent energies. I know this because I do it all the time and very rarely does my instinct let me down. We have observed Luke walk into a room and gravitate towards certain individuals, and without fail he always picks the people who have had to stand strong against adversity. He will walk away from people who are not pure in their thoughts and actions. He does not tolerate their energy on any level. Thankfully, Desmond completely understood this whole way of being without me having to explain anything, and as a result Resistance Day came and swiftly disappeared. I was relieved and amazed.

Two hours later I returned to pick Luke up and he relaxed back into the new calm and controlled Luke with each hour that passed. He had a huge lunch which certainly helped and then we went on another adventure to the CN Tower in Toronto.

Forty-eight hours ago we had carried out the same train journey to Toronto but this time there was a difference. Luke was so in control of his body and actions that he barely sat on my knees on the train or held my hand walking from the station to the CN Tower. He followed all of my instructions first time and just looked so much more peaceful than previously. Considering that this was 'resistance day', all was going extremely well. Luke and I thoroughly enjoyed going up the elevator at lightning speed in the CN Tower and looking through the glass floor. While we were on the train Luke called me 'Mum' for the second time and in my world that's a pattern as it was more than once. Luke is changing in so many ways, and I cannot say 'in even more ways than I expected,' as I arrived ten days ago with no agenda, no expectation... just a whole load of hope.

We returned to our hotel and Luke very purposefully took me to the movie room and so I removed his NOIT so he could readjust and get ready to fall asleep. By 8:00 p.m. he was sound asleep and his face and body looked very relaxed. Remember, getting Luke to fall asleep has not been an easy task in the past.

It's fascinating watching Luke move through the developmental milestones of a 2-3 year old, and as a result becoming more independent. It's the speed at which it's all happening that is incredibly exciting. Luke looks different. He has grown taller and broader and his chest and shoulders have expanded. His face has changed and he now looks like a relaxed young six-year-old boy.

I cannot express how overwhelming it is to be surrounded by such brilliant people who are doing whatever they can to help unlock Luke and make each day the best it can possibly be. For many years my husband and I have had to drive absolutely everything by following our intuition, which has been both daunting and fearful. I feel like I'm riding one big wave, surrounded by brilliant, kind, caring and professional people, that are sweeping Luke and me down the right path. This is how life should be. People with brilliant ideas and a desire to make a difference to those individuals who need it the most should be empowered to just get on with what they do best – even if their ideas are new.

*Day #10: **Relearning to Play***

Luke decided at 3:00 a.m. it was time to wake up, a two-hour improvement on the previous two mornings so I saw that as progress! Thankfully he fell asleep again around 4:30 a.m. and by 7:00 a.m. I was preparing another strong coffee.

We arrived at Desmond's for 9:00 a.m. and Luke was so excited he couldn't contain himself. He just ran to the nearest front door (they all look the same) in his hunt for Desmond. He suddenly saw Desmond out of the corner of his eye and in his excitement and speed Luke slipped off the curb. He immediately looked painfully into my eyes. It had hurt him, but after a quick hug he impatiently grabbed our backpack as if to say, "Just get me into Desmond's office now!", so in we went. Despite always looking like he is going to fall over, Luke's balance is very good. However Desmond and I have both observed Luke exploring with his balance in the last few days. Yesterday morning he walked on the balls of his feet and the day before that he appeared to be seeing how far forward he could lean before falling over, and nine times out of ten he would catch himself. Witnessing Luke explore his new world is just fascinating and for once (with the insight of Desmond) I have an idea as to what Luke is trying to work out. I am beginning to understand Luke much, much more which makes me feel incredibly blessed.

Not too long ago when I had visited a physician, we had a conversation that revolved around the sudden changes in Luke from such a bright, sparky, and independent baby to the silent young boy he was then. She asked me if I felt I had grieved for the loss of my son. At the time I found this question far too upsetting to answer, but if truth be told, yes, I had – and more than once – due to the significant regression in Luke since he was two years old. Today I realized that I am no longer feeling that unbearable and excruciating pain of not understanding my own son, yet absolutely loving getting to know him once again. That is why I feel so very blessed. So, on Day 10, I left Luke safely with Desmond and they were going to work on turn taking, visit the park, go and buy some more groceries, and visit the local fire station.

When I returned to pick up Luke, Desmond told me that Luke had loved the fire station and that we should go back, so off we went. Desmond was right. Luke did love it! He really explored the fire engines. He opened every single door, sat in every single seat and even had a go at pretending to drive the fire engine. Luke was actually beginning to role play – he's never done that. We have taken him and his brother to places where they can sit in trucks, tractors, and fire engines, but Luke has never shown any interest in any of them. It was just a wonderful moment. The NOIT was now helping Luke to really play within his new surroundings and this small example shows how he's getting more and more comfortable with what his eyes and ears are telling him!

Luke was starving again during his morning session. This is a good sign though, as Luke's body is using up so much energy processing his new world that he needs to maintain his food intake to continue taking everything in. This leads me onto the next developmental milestone we're working through and relearning. Luke's eating habits are not the best. He can use a fork when he wants to but he would much prefer to just use his fingers. Desmond demonstrated how I should reteach Luke this core skill and already after one day I can see this difference. I am on such a journey myself.

This afternoon I took Luke to a local hairdresser following a recommendation from Desmond. Honestly, I nearly cried (again!) as the difference from Luke getting his hair cut back home to today was another transformation. First, I did have the iPad playing in the distance to entertain Luke, which is our usual tactic. However, he didn't move, I didn't need to touch him to make sure he stayed in his seat. He stayed perfectly still apart from when some hairs went in his eyes. At points,

Luke smiled broadly as he liked the clippers on his head and at the end of the haircut he returned to his seat for more! The hairdresser was absolutely brilliant. She worked quickly and her jovial, gentle words of encouragement had the perfect mix. I left the hair salon incredibly pleased.

After a quick swim and bath we left to go and have dinner at Dr. Cathy's and her husband Ron's house with Desmond. I was really excited as I thoroughly enjoy talking to them all, observing Desmond's strategies with Luke, and Luke's reactions to these strategies. I always feel incredibly relaxed in their company and tonight was no exception. We learned Luke loves sushi! We also saw his sense of humour beginning to return and I gained such insight into his non-verbal cues with Desmond talking me through them and my options. Luke kept taking myself and Desmond back to the car whenever we went on a walk with him – he was telling us he was done – so we followed his lead and said our goodbyes.

Yeeeeeeesssss, Luke slept in until 6.30 a.m.! All new mums with small children will know that feeling of when their child finally sleeps through the night for the first time – you feel even worse than you did when being woken up in the night because you're not used to the deep sleep. Well, that was me this morning! However, I take any sleep I can get and Luke certainly looked so much better for it.

This morning we met Desmond downstairs in the lobby of our hotel, which was different for Luke and purposely arranged to encourage Luke to get used to seeing Desmond in different locations. Luke immediately grabbed Desmond's hand, spotted his car and led Desmond to it. Luke was ready to go off on his adventure.

Desmond had another great morning with Luke, although Des noticed after a few moments in the car that Luke didn't look right. Des removed his headrest from the front passenger seat so Luke could see right out of the front window which immediately perked him up. He was once again alert and taking everything in. Des explained that trying to orient yourself sideways on with cars whizzing past you is really tricky when you sit on one side of the car. Needless to say I moved our car seat and Luke now sits proudly observing the views around him while being well oriented. It's the small acts that make the big difference to Luke.

This morning Desmond met us outside our hotel because we were off to the local swimming pool as this is Luke's favourite hobby. I had the privilege of joining Luke and Desmond this morning and I had a great time. This morning was all about seeing how Luke coped without the NOIT.

Luke started the day by wearing the NOIT and he was very attentive and focused. When we arrived at the swimming pool, we explored the four ice rinks which Luke insisted in going into despite wearing only shorts and a t-shirt. Luke and I got changed in the family changing room, and normally I have to take Luke into a cubicle with the door locked; otherwise he just runs wild around the changing room. Because of how calm and in control Luke was I decided to take a chance and we got ready in the main changing room area (it was a big space). Once again, Luke impressed me so much as he got undressed (with some help) and then picked up his bag and held it peacefully while he waited for me to get ready. It was incredible and so much so I caught myself wondering how on earth we have coped with the previous ways when getting ready to go swimming. I know the answer is 'that you just do because you have to,' but I had such a pleasurable experience just getting ready and we hadn't even entered the pool yet.

Also, I noticed I really tensed up when I had to take the NOIT *off Luke. I caught myself thinking, "My goodness, I must have been in that tense state for so long now that I didn't feel or notice it." I once again felt the relief I mentioned earlier in the week. I took a deep breath and removed the* NOIT *from Luke so we could go in the swimming pool. Desmond fitted Luke with a life jacket as he wanted Luke to be as independent as possible as well as enjoy the feeling of floating around. Desmond explained that when he trained to be a Davis Facilitator he wore the* NOIT *from 8:00 a.m. to 5:00 p.m. as he wanted to gain a thorough understanding of how it felt from his client's perspective. He explained that when Luke wears the* NOIT *he is never given the opportunity to 'switch off'. The* NOIT's *'tinging' sound repeats every eight seconds to support natural orientation. Although Luke seems incredibly content with this constant refocus, it is exhausting for him, and Desmond knew this because he had first-hand experience.*

Once in the pool, Luke had a fabulous time and explored the pool for approximately 45 minutes. Desmond and I witnessed Luke watching the fountain from the side of the pool with great intent. For the first time Luke was linking objects. For example, he liked placing his hands at the beginning of the fountain, but slowly he then noticed the opposite side where the fountain landed in the pool. He swam from one side to another while observing the water making the arch in between. He was linking objects together and working it out in his own mind. We have been waiting for Luke to begin to link objects together/break them down for a long time and it was great to see him think, "Right, it starts there, goes over my head and lands here!" Luke loved the water jets and pumps – they must have been providing him with some sort of sensory therapy. Again, this reminded me that Luke's sensory needs have significantly reduced during our time here. I couldn't believe I hadn't spotted this before now. Luke's sensory needs have always been excruciatingly high. The NOIT has significantly reduced his need for constant sensory feedback. He's beginning to use his other senses (smell, touch, hearing and taste) to help him figure out our world – just awesome!

We then enjoyed a warm shower and Desmond took us for brunch at a nearby cafe. Desmond modelled to me the importance of actively encouraging Luke to orient himself around his new surroundings by going for a little walk around. When we arrived, Luke really struggled to settle and sit in his seat, even when wearing the NOIT. As soon as Desmond explained that Luke needs to feel completely settled with this new building before we sit down and eat, I got it and it was all so simple – yet I hadn't appreciated the importance of this strategy until that moment. I am honestly learning so much and thriving in being shown how to understand my new role in helping meet Luke's needs. Luke demolished a real treat of a crepe with Nutella, strawberries, bananas and whipped cream.

Later that day we drove to the Toronto Zoo, and on the way Luke enjoyed another afternoon nap. I then realized he's had a nap in the car most afternoons. This is something a toddler would do, reinforcing where Luke is at the moment in terms of his developmental milestones. He hasn't napped in the day since he was about two years old and it really isn't a coincidence. The zoo was so peaceful that it was perfect for Luke. We immediately headed for the KidsZone and for the first time I witnessed Luke 'playing' on the equipment and having fun with exploring it all. I could see him working things out really clearly and then tackling some of the obstacles. He enjoyed climbing over them all, going through them or under them. He cheekily climbed back up a tube slide (he knows he's not allowed to do this) and when he saw me up at the top he grinned and slid back down.

Eventually we moved on to the pandas. Normally Luke pays no attention to the animals and just walks on right past. Today was different. He noticed the pandas, especially the male panda, and watched him for a good few moments, I'm sure I saw a smile when he saw him wrestling with the bamboo sticks. I was thrilled that Luke appeared interested to see the panda.

It got even better when we saw the orangutan close up; she was really close to us and did a really big stretch while lying down. I am certain Luke imitated her actions as his arms gently went into the air just like hers. So on a high we returned to the car and made our way home.

Unbelievably Luke slept from 7:30 p.m. until 7:15 a.m. I, however, woke up at 3:00 a.m., 4:00.a.m., and 5.a.m. expecting my morning hug!

Final Day

Today was all about 'handover day. I woke up incredibly anxious, full of questions/concerns, some of which I have listed below:

What if I can't continue this progress at home?

What if I get it wrong?

Who's going to help me in my moments of need?

I don't want to be on my own again.

I don't want to deal with the 'doubters.

Just generally feeling 'AAARRRGGGHHHH!!'

I felt an overwhelming sense of fear about stepping into the plane to go home tomorrow because of the above. However, I swiftly discovered, within an hour of meeting Desmond, I really didn't need to have any fear.

First Desmond talked me through the Stepping Stones Program he has been working toward with Luke and explained the finer intricacies. He taught me how to set my 'energy dial' which is now (and probably has always been; I just didn't appreciate it) so critical for Luke to cope with everyday life.

Desmond then taught me the 'release' procedure which is achieved through a particular breathing method. I have witnessed Luke's whole being change within seconds of Desmond doing the breathing techniques with him, as it helps Luke regulate his body and mimics the effect of the NOIT to a certain extent. Desmond talked me through the release and I fell into a bit of a meditative state during these few moments, so was able to appreciate the power of this breathing method on Luke. No wonder he relaxes immediately.

Beth, Director of NOIT Research, then arrived and she talked through the development of the NOIT and the impact it's had on individuals to date. I could listen to Beth for hours, but the one thing I was struggling with was the question, "Why on earth is the NOIT technology not well known far and wide?" I asked Beth this question and she explained that individuals around the world have had great success once the NOIT has been introduced and those individuals have been incredibly pleased with the outcomes as a result of using the NOIT. They, of course, tell others but that's where it stops. Beth then explained how unique Luke's journey has been in relation to the speed at which he has progressed before our very eyes. Usually clients have approximately one-hour weekly sessions with a Davis Autism Approach facilitator, and although progress is always achieved it is at a slower pace – understandably.

The difference with Luke is that we've immersed ourselves in his progress 24/7 and embraced every opportunity to maximise the outcome of using the NOIT. In addition Luke and Desmond are the perfect combination. We have struck magic here and that has been crucial to Luke's progress. They have a special bond that was obvious from the very first moment they met and cemented within 20 minutes of meeting. Due to the intensive time they have been together Desmond has been able to really pull on Luke's interests and make rapid gains. In addition we are an 'all or nothing' kind of family and never do anything by half measures. That in itself has contributed to the success of our two weeks. We arrived with hope and pure intentions, and then ran with every opportunity that presented itself. I am certain that gave Luke the permission to accept this invitation to jump in and see what happens. Luke felt safe so he was prepared to take those bold and brave steps to tackle this new world.

Desmond had then arranged for us all to speak with Heidi Rose, who is a Davis Autism Facilitator in Australia, and has a great deal of experience working with non-verbal children and the NOIT in conjunction with the Davis Autism Approach. Heidi was a fountain of knowledge and made it very clear as to what I need to focus on when we return home tomorrow. I have to remember that although Luke is six years old, he is developmentally working through the stages of a two-and-a-half to three-year-old. This means I need to treat him as though he is six years old. Patronizing Luke is definitely not the way forward, yet I need to remember where he is developmentally and so make sure certain aspects of his life are age-appropriate to ensure he can master certain skills to move forward. I understand this fact far better than I can write it down. Heidi was very clear that whatever I do I need to triangulate it on a physical level, a thought level, and an energy level. We do this naturally with a toddler but I really need to embrace it all of the time with Luke to support him while he works through his developmental milestones.

Heidi also made a really valid point that I hadn't considered before. This is Luke's second chance and he's learning everything from scratch. Heidi explained that when we return home everything will be new to Luke, as he will be seeing everything for the first time in an oriented state. This will begin from the moment we step into the car, drive up to our house, walk through the front door, and into his bedroom. I've been very aware that Luke's been learning everything for the first time here, but everything was new so it was easier for me to appreciate that I needed to explain everything to him. I hadn't considered this for when we get home.

Desmond, you are a marvel and you have saved us and our gorgeous boy from despair. You have shown him that life can be good and fun. Thank you for just being you, being the eternal optimist and seeing the potential in Luke even before you had met him. All in all, this trip has been life changing. Luke is waking up again and in full flow. I believe the keys have been found.

Luke has continued to make progress, and at the time of this writing had spent two more weeks working with Desmond half-days, and his vocabulary was up to approximately 45 words.

He had gone from putting clay into his mouth every time Des introduced it, to recognizing that clay models could represent objects and people in the real world, to helping create models, perhaps by assisting Desmond to put the head on a body, or point to a specific model or part of a model.

It is important to stress here that not all children progress as quickly as Luke, and not all react as dramatically to the NOIT as Luke did. Some individuals are only willing to begin wearing the NOIT or listening to the 'ting' sound through headphones for a few minutes or hours at a time. The minute the individual indicates he has had enough for that time, off it comes, so the process can take a lot longer.

What Desmond was doing was getting Luke ready for the Davis Stepping Stones Program. Before that program can begin, a person with ASD needs to be oriented enough to follow simple directions, have enough communication skills to understand what is happening when clay models are being used, and be able to participate in the program as described earlier. Luke is on his way.

PART FIVE
What is Autism Today?

What is autism? The answer to that question depends a little on who you ask and when you ask. In the past, there have been various names for this condition, including autism, Asperger's Syndrome, high-functioning autism, autism spectrum disorder, autistic disorder, and pervasive developmental disorder-not otherwise specified.

The most widely used medical diagnostic criteria in North America are found in the Diagnostic and Statistical Manual of Mental Disorders (DSM), published and regularly updated by the American Psychiatric Association. In its fourth edition, DSM-IV, the criteria for autistic disorder, under the umbrella of pervasive developmental disorder, included: impairment in social interaction; impairment in communication; and restricted, repetitive, and stereotyped patterns of behaviour, interests and activities. DSM-IV also provides criteria with which to determine whether an individual meets the threshold within each of these categories required for diagnosis. Additional related disorders, with the same impairments but with differing levels of impairment, or differing ages of onset, included Asperger's disorder, childhood disintegrative disorder, and pervasive developmental disorder-not otherwise specified (American Psychiatric Association 1994).

In the latest edition, DSM-5, released in 2013, all of these separate disorders are consolidated into one diagnostic category: autism spectrum disorder (ASD).

Criteria for autism spectrum disorder in DSM-5 are listed below. In each section, first (A, B, C...) are broad categories. Second (1, 2, 3 ...) are how these categories are to be interpreted, and third (a, b, c ...) are specific examples of how these behaviours may be observed.

A. Persistent deficits in social communication and social interaction across contexts, not accounted for by general developmental delays, and manifested by <u>all three</u> of the following:

1. Deficits in social-emotional reciprocity ranging from abnormal social approach and failure of normal back-and-forth conversation through reduced sharing of interests, emotions, affect, and response, to total lack of initiation of social interaction.

   a. Relative failure to initiate or sustain conversational interchange (at whatever level of language skills are present) in which there is no reciprocal to and from responsiveness to the communications of the other person

   b. Lack of shared enjoyment in terms of vicarious plea-sure in other people's happiness and/or a spontaneous seeking to share their own enjoyment through joint involvement with others

   c.   Markedly impaired awareness of others

   d.   Lack of social-emotional reciprocity

2. Deficits in nonverbal communicative behaviours used for social interaction ranging from poorly integrated verbal and nonverbal communication, through abnormalities in eye contact and body-language, or deficits in understanding and use of nonverbal communication, to total lack of facial expression or gestures

   a.   Markedly abnormal nonverbal communication, as in the use of eye-to-eye gaze, facial expression, body posture or gestures to initiate or modulate social interaction (e.g. does not anticipate being held, stiffens when held, does not greet parents or visitors, has a fixed stare in social situations)

3. Deficits in developing and maintaining relationships appropriate to developmental level (beyond those with caregivers) ranging from difficulties adjusting behaviour to suit different social contexts, through difficulties in sharing imaginative play and in making friends, to an apparent absence of interest in people

a. Failure to develop peer relationships as appropriate to developmental level

b. No or abnormal social play (e.g. does not actively participate in simple games; prefers solitary play activities; involves other children in play only as "mechanical aids")

B. Restricted, repetitive patterns of behaviours, interests, or activities as manifested by at least two of the following:

1. Stereotyped or repetitive speech, motor movements, or use of objects; (such as simple motor stereotypies[3], echolalia[4], repetitive use of objects, or idiosyncratic phrases)

   a. Stereotyped and repetitive use of language or idiosyncratic language

   b. Stereotyped body movements

2. Excessive adherence to routines, ritualized patterns of verbal or nonverbal behaviour, or excessive resistance to change; (such as motoric rituals, insistence on same route or food, repetitive questioning, or extreme distress at small changes)

---

3 Persistent repetition or sameness of acts, ideas, or words

4 Automatic repetition of vocalizations made by another person

a. Apparently compulsive adherence to specific non-functional rituals or routines

b. Distress over changes in small, non-functional details of the environment

3. Highly restricted, fixated interests that are abnormal in intensity or focus; (such as strong attachment to or preoccupation with unusual objects, excessively circumscribed or perseverative interests)

a. An encompassing preoccupation with stereotyped and restricted patterns of interest

4. Hyper- or hyporeactivity to sensory input or unusual interest in sensory aspects of environment; (such as apparent indifference to pain/heat/cold, adverse response to specific sounds or textures, excessive smelling or touching of objects, fascination with lights or spinning objects)

a. Hyper- or hyporeactivity to sensory stimuli e.g. hyperacusis[5]

C. Symptoms must be present in early childhood (but may not become fully manifest until social demands exceed limited capacities)

---

5 An over-sensitivity to certain frequency ranges of sound

1. Abnormal development prior to age three as manifested by delays or abnormal functioning in social development, language as used in social communication, or play

2. Onset by 36 months

D. Symptoms together limit and impair everyday functioning

The rationale behind the change in diagnostic criteria was that the previous separate diagnoses were not consistently applied across different clinics and treatment centres. It was possible for individuals to qualify for services in some jurisdictions but not others, depending on which subcategory they fell into, and whether those categories were recognized in their place of residence or not.

It is postulated that the new criteria will enable better diagnoses at different ages.

Despite these claims, there is some concern that a significant number of individuals diagnosed under DSM IV criteria would no longer be included under the new ASD criteria, and therefore no longer be eligible for services. In one study evaluating the potential impact of the changes, it was found that a substantial portion (39.4%) of individuals with those ASDs other than autistic disorder would be excluded (McPartland 2012). The most affected would be those previously diagnosed with Asperger's Disorder and PDD-NOS.

Autism Canada lists the primary symptoms of autism as:

- impaired communication;

- impaired social skills;
- perseveration on interests and activities.

Additional characteristics listed by Autism Canada include:
– abnormal responses to sensory stimulation;
– variability of intellectual functioning;
– uneven development profile;
– dependence on routine;
– behaviour problems;
– difficulties in sleeping, toileting, and eating;
– immune irregularities;
– gastrointestinal deficiencies;
– nutritional deficiencies.

Autism Canada also lists the following strengths often observed in children with ASD at levels beyond expectations for their age.
– non-verbal reasoning skills;
– reading skills;
– perceptual motor skills;
– drawing skills;
– computer interests and skills;
– exceptional memory;
– visual-spatial abilities;
– music skills

In summary, ASD is characterized by a core triad of impairments in social skills, impairments in communication skills, and limited or repetitive interests and behaviours.

Social skills development is variable. In some, there continues to be little or no awareness that other people even exist, while in others, social skills may be relatively well developed, but continue to be an area of challenge. In his wonderful book, *Be different: Adventures of a Free-Range Aspergian*, John Elder Robinson (Robinson 2011) describes the extent to which social situations still require his deliberate attention and processing. He tells how he used to go into a room where others were watching TV and change the channel to the program he wanted to watch. He was always mystified when the others were annoyed at his self-centred action. Now when he goes into a room, he makes a point of noticing the people in the room and what they are doing. He might still change the channel, but he knows now to make some comment about it that acknowledges what he is doing may seem rude to them; it is better than not noticing what he is doing, and often the others agree, even if reluctantly, to the channel change with much better resulting social relationships.

Speech development is often impaired, and in some non-verbal individuals with ASD, it never develops. In others, speech can develop to a very high level. In either case, and at all levels in between, people with ASD continue to experience some difficulties in using language effectively for social communication. Children with ASD can sound like *little professors* when discussing an area of special interest, but sound stilted and often be off-topic in general social conversation.

Repetitive and stereo-typical behaviours, or limited interests and behaviours, similarly vary widely. Behaviours can run from self-stimulating actions such as self-biting, head-banging, or picking at skin, to hand flapping, rocking, echolalia, or twirling. When interests are limited, an individual with ASD may talk endlessly about topics that are of little interest to the people around him. He may resist doing anything that is not directly tied to his area of interest.

The fourth item within the second criterion (see B, 4, a) of DSM-5 relates to sensory processing disorders:

Hyper or hyporeactivity to sensory stimuli

According to some researchers (Tomchek 2007), up to 95% of people with ASD can be shown to have Unusual Sensory Experiences (USEs). Leekam and colleagues (Leekham 2007) found that adverse sensory reactions occur in at least 90% of individuals with ASD. One analysis of several studies indicates that USE's occur across all ages and degrees of severity of ASD (Ben-Sasson, Hen and Engel-Yeger 2009).

With these findings, it may be arguable that this should be a separate category, rather than being lumped in as one example of "restricted or repetitive patterns of behaviour." It certainly raises some interesting questions about the role sensory abnormalities might play in other key characteristics of ASD.

Social skills deficits is one of the primary characteristics of ASD. Smith and Sharp, in a study of adults with Asperger Syndrome, discovered that USEs are frequently at the root of social problems leading to isolation (Smith 2013). They reported that a common issue emerging from many qualitative studies is 'peculiar perceptions.' Their literature review led to several conclusions such as:

- The severity of sensory processing problems is correlated with poorer behavioural, emotional and adaptive functioning.
- Poor sensory processing is correlated with more severe
  autistic symptoms.
- Perceptual processing dysfunction remains a core symptom
  of autism throughout the lifespan.

They found that the most common action taken by individuals with ASD when dealing with sensory overload was to escape the source of the stress. This appeared to be not a choice, but more like an 'irresistible compulsion.' This behaviour is usually interpreted as poor social functioning, and results in rejection. Over time, the adults in the study reported decreasing inclination to venture into situations where sensory overload *might* be encountered, thus resulting in social isolation. Routine, predictability, and control were seen as ways of managing the stress related to USEs.

Repetitive and restricted actions and interests are a key aspect of autism. There is some indication that these behaviours may be secondary to USEs. Smith & Sharp (2012) found that repetitive behaviours are used by adults with Asperger Syndrome (AS) to calm themselves and reduce the stress of USEs. A correlation has also been found between the degree of sensory abnormalities and the amount of restricted and repetitive behaviours in children with ASD (Chen, Rodgers & McConachie, 2009).

I think this issue provides a key to explaining why the Davis approach works so well.

If you or your loved one has difficulties in the core triad of communication impairments, social skills impairments, and limited or repetitive interests/behaviour, you might want to look into an assessment to determine whether a diagnosis of autism spectrum disorder would be appropriate.

Some people are resistant to labelling, and prefer to think it is better simply to provide the assistance and resources that will help the individual. I have never been one of those people. I believe knowledge is power. I often tell people that I would never let a doctor near my face with a scalpel in hand without first understanding the nature of the tissue she is about to cut out, and what other treatment options might be available to me. If that requires getting a diagnosis of skin cancer, then I want to know what kind of skin cancer, and I want to know what other treatments might be possible. A diagnosis of ASD, ADHD, or dyslexia is no different. It provides a good starting point to discuss options and solutions. Smith and Sharp report that for some of the adults with Asperger's Syndrome in their study, knowing their diagnosis of AS appeared to be key in helping them and others, such as their caregivers, cope with difficult situations (Smith 2013).

Although there is some controversy about the incidence of ASD, there is agreement that the incidence is increasing rapidly. On its web site, Autism Speaks Canada says 2012 numbers reflect a 78% increase in diagnoses in the past six years. They provide 2013 numbers indicating one in 88 children have ASD, and one in 54 boys. These figures are consistent with a report from the US Centre for Disease Control and Prevention (CDC) (Baio 2012), although the report cautions that these figures cannot be assumed to reflect national norms, as they were gathered from only 14 sites, and within those sites, statistics fluctuated significantly.

There are also differing opinions regarding the reason for the sharp increase in diagnosed cases of ASD, including better diagnostic protocols, increased awareness, environmental triggers, and more treatment options.

APPENDIX I

Structure and Timing of a Davis Autism Approach Program

Structure: The three parts of a Davis Autism Approach Program have been described in the text.

The most typical scenario is that the program is delivered by a trained and certified Davis Autism Approach facilitator/coach. In that case, the client works with the facilitator at times convenient for the facilitator and the client/client's family. A typical scenario would be for the facilitator and client to work in one-week blocks, usually from 9:00 a.m.–4:00 p.m. This continues until all parts of the program have been completed, with a break of two or three months between the Identity Development segment and the Social Integration Segment.

One alternative format is for the program to be delivered by a parent or loved one as a coached program. In this case, the facilitator gets the client started, completing the Individuation segment of the program and introducing the client to the concept mastery procedure. The facilitator then works with the person (helper) who will continue to work with the client, making sure the helper has mastered the tools, the concept mastery procedure, and the client's next several concepts. Then the helper and client continue to work at the client's home until those concepts have been mastered. The client returns to the facilitator for a day or two to begin the next group of concepts, then the facilitator walks the helper through the remaining concepts in the group, and the client and helper continue to work through those concepts at home. This continues until the Identity Development Segment of the program is complete, with the facilitator available to consult or assist as necessary. The client returns to the facilitator to complete the Social Integration portion of the program.

A third option is for the parent or family member, or a professional who has a good working relationship with the client, to attend a five-day workshop called Davis Life Concepts for Autism. In this workshop, the parent or other helper will learn how to work with one individual with ASD to complete the Davis Autism Approach Program at home. For information about Davis Autism Workshops, go to www.davisautism.com

Because the Davis Autism Approach Program can be done with anyone age eight or older, the timing can vary significantly. The program is always done at the speed appropriate to the individual client, and therefore it is not possible to predict how long a program might require. In most cases, a program can be completed in anywhere from two weeks to five weeks. The Social Integration segment requires about three additional days. This would be based on a 30-hour work week. If the program is done in half-days, the number of weeks would be doubled. When a program is done as a coached program, or done by a parent or helper at home, it can be worked into the client's days as possible, and the time is dictated by the pace.

Davis Stepping Stones is appropriate for children under the age of eight, or for those with very limited or no language. It is an introduction to the Davis Autism Approach Program. Because one cannot begin with the concepts until the client has enough language to understand instructions and follow directions, Stepping Stones takes much longer. This is the program Luke was introduced to, and it takes as long as it takes for language and focus to be ready for the Davis Autism Approach Program. You can find details at www.davisautism.com

REFERENCES

Alderson, J. *Challenging the Myths of Autism: Unlock New Possibiliites and Hope.* Toronto: HarperCollins, 2011.

American Psychiatric Association. *Diagnostic and Statistical Manual, Fourth Edition.* American Psychiatric Association, 1994.

Diaignostic and Statistical Manual of Mental Disorders, 4th edition; text revision TR. Washington DC: American Psychiatric Association, 2000.

Attwood, Tony. *The Complete Guide to Asperger Syndrome.* London and Philidelphia: Jessica Kingsley Publishers Ltd., 2006.

Baio, Jon. *Prevalence of Autism Spectrum Disorder - Autism and Developmental Disablities Monitoring Network, 14 Sites, United States, 2008.* Centres for Disease Control and Prevention, 2012.

Baldwin, D. "Infants' contribution to the achievement of joint reference." *Child Development, 62,* 1991: 875-890.

Baron-Cohan, S. "Do people with autism understand what causes emotion?" *Child Development, 62,* 1991: 385-395.

Baron-Cohan, S. "Out of sight or out of mind: another look at deception in autism." *Journal of Child Psychology and Psychiatry, 33,* 1992: 1141-1155.

Baron-Cohen, S. "Are autistic children behaviourists? An examination of their mental-physical and appearance-reality distinctions." *Journal of Autism and Developmental Disorders, 19,* 1989a: 579-600.

Baron-Cohen, S. "Autism and symbolic play." *British Journal of Developmental Psychology, 5,* 1987: 139-148.

Baron-Cohen, S. "Hey! It was just a joke! Understanding propositions and propositional attitudes by normally developing children and children with autism." *Israel Journal of Psychiatry, 34,* 1997: 174-178.

Baron-Cohen, S. "Perceptual role-taking and protodeclarative pointing in autism." *British Journal of Developmental Psychology, 7,* 1989c: 113-127.

Baron-Cohen, S. "Social and pragmatic deficits in autism: cognitive or affective?" *Journal of Autism and Developmental Disorders, 18,* 1988: 379-402.

Baron-Cohen, S. "The autistic child's theory of mind: a case of specific developmental delay." *Journal of Child Psychology and Psychiatry, 30,* 1989b: 285-298.

Baron-Cohen, S., & Cross, P. "Reading the eyes: evidence for the role of perception in the development of a theory of mind." *Mind and Language,6,* 1992: 173-186.

Baron-Cohen, S., & Goodhart, F. "The "seeing leads to knowing" deficit in autism: the Pratt and Bryant probe." *British Journal of Developmental Psychology, 12*, 1994: 397-402.

Baron-Cohen, S., & Hammer, J. "Parents of children with Asperger Syndrome: what is the cognitive phenotype?" *Journal of Cognitive Neuroscience, 9*, 1997: 548-554.

Baron-Cohen, S., Baldwin, D., & Crowson, M. "Do children with autism use the Speaker's Direction of Gaze (SDG) strategy to crack the code of language?" *Child Development, 68*, 1997a: 48-57.

Baron-Cohen, S., Campbell, R., Karmiloff-Smith, A., Grant, J., & Walker, J. "Are children with autism blind to the mentalistic significance of the eyes?" *British Journal of Developmental Psychology, 13*, 1995: 379-398.

Baron-Cohen, S., Cox, A., Baird, G., Swettenham, J., Drew, A., Nightengale, N., Morgan, K., & Charman, T. "Psychological markers of autism at 18 months of age in a large population." *British Journal of Psychiatry, 168*, 1996: 158-163.

Baron-Cohen, S., Jolliffe, T., Mortimer, C., & Robertson, M. "Another advanced test of theory of mind: evidence from very high functioning adults with autism or Asperger Syndrome." *Journal of Child Psychology and Psychiatry, 38*, 1997: 813-822.

Baron-Cohen, S., Leslie, A.M., & Frith, U. "Does the autistic child have a 'theory of mind'?" *Cognition, 21*, 1985: 37-46.

Baron-Cohen, S., Leslie, A.M., & Frith, U. "Mechanical, behavioural and intentional understanding of picture stories in autistic children." *British Journal of Developmental Psychology, 4,* 1986: 113-125.

Baron-Cohen, S., O'Riordan, M., Stone, V., Jones, R., & Plaisted, K. "Recogniton of faux pas by normally developing children and children with Asperger Syndrome or high-functioning autism." *Journal of Autism and Developmental Disorders, 29,* 1999a: 407-418.

Baron-Cohen, S., Ring, H., Moriarty, J., Shmitz, P., Costa, D., & Ell, P. "Recognition of mental state terms: a clinical study of autism and functionall neuroimaging study of normal adults." *British Journal of Psychiatry, 165,* 1994: 640-649.

Baron-Cohen, S., Spitz, A., & Cross, P. "Can children with autism recognize surprise?" *Cognition and Emotion,* 1993: 507-516.

Baron-Cohen, S., Wheelwright, S., & Jollife, T. "Is there a "language ot the eyes"? Evidence from normal adults and adults with autism or Asperger syndrome." *Visual Cognition, 4,* 1997c: 311-331.

Baron-Cohen, S., Wheelwright, S., Stone, V., & Rutherford, M. "A mathematician, a physicist, and a computer scientist with Asperger Syndrome: performance on folk psychology and folk physics test." *Neurocase, 5,* 1999b: 475-483.

Ben-Sasson, Ayelet, L., Fluss, R., Cermak, S. A. Hen, and B., and Gal, E. Engel-Yeger. "A Meta-Analysis of Sensory Modulation Symptoms in Individuals with Autism Spectrum Disorders." *Journal of Autism and Developmental Disorders (39)*, 2009: 1-11.

Bowler, D. M. "'Theory of Mind' in Asperger Syndrome." *Journal of Child Psychology and Psychiatry, 33*, 1992: 877-895.

Butterworth, G., & Jarrett, N. "What minds have in common is space: spatial mechanisms serving joint attention in infancy." *British Journal of Developmental Psychology, 9*, 1991: 55-72.

Chen, Yu-Han, Jacqui Rodgers, & Helen McConachie. "Restricted and Repetitive Behaviors, Sensory Processing and Cognitive Style n Children with Autism Spectrum Disorders." *Journal of Autism and Developmental Disorders, 39*, 2009: 635-642.

Chickering, Alexander W., and Linda Reisser. *Education and Identity (2nd ed.)*. San Francisco, CA: Jossey-Bass, 1993.

Davis, Ronald D. *Nurturing the Seed of Genius: Davis Autism Approach (TM) Manual*. Burlingame: Davis Dyslexia Asociation International, 2007.

—. *Nurturing the Seed of Genius: Faciltators Workshop Manual*. Burlingame CA: Davis Autism Association International, 2009.

Davis, Ronald D. with Eldon M. Braun. *The Gift of Dyslexia: Why Some of the Smartest People Can't Read...and How They Can Learn*. New York: Penguin Group, 2010.

Erikson, Erik H. *Childhood and Society.* New York: W W Norton & Company, 1993.

Flavell, H., Green, E.R., & Flavell, E.R. "Development of knowledge about the appearance-reality distinction." *Society for Research in Child Development,* 1986: 51.

Frith, U., Happe, F., & Siddons, F. "Autism and theory of mind in everyday life." *Social eEvelopment, 3,* 1994: 108-124.

Hadwin, J., Baron-Cohen, S., Howlin, P. & Hill, K. "Can we teach children with autism to understand emotions, belief, or pretence?" *Development and Psychopathology, 8,* 1996: 345-365.

Happe, F. "An advanced test of theory of mind: Understanding of story characters' thoughts and feelings by able autistic, mentally handicapped, and normal children and adults." *Journal of Autism and Developmental Disorders, 24,* 1994: 129-154.

Happe, F. "Communicative competence and theory of mind in autism: A Test of Relevance Theory." *Cognition, 48,* 1993: 101-119.

Happe, F. "The role of age and verbal ability in the theory of mind task performance of subjects with autism." *Child Development, 66,* 1995: 843-855.

Korkmaz, Baris. "Theory of Mind and Neurodevelopmental Disorders of Childhood." *Neuropsychiatric Disorders and Pediatric Psychiatry,* 2011: 101R-108R.

Leekham, S., Nieto, C., Libby, S., Wing, L. & Gould, J. "Describing the sensory abnormalities of children and adults with autism." *Journal of Autism and Developmental Disorders, 37(5)*, 2007: 894-910.

Marshall, Abigail with Ronald D. Davis. *Autism and the Seeds of Change.* USA, 2012.

Maslow, Abraham H. *Toward a Psychology of Being, 3rd edition.* USA: John Wiley & Sons, 1999.

McPartland, J. C., Reichow, B., & Volkman, F. R. "Sensitivity and Specificity of Proposed DSM-5 Diagnostic Criteria for Autism Spectrum Disorder." *Journal of the American Academy of Child & Adolescent Psychiatry*, 2012: Vol.51, Issue 4, p368-383.

Pert, Candace. *Molecules of Emotion.* New york: Simon & Schuster, 1999.

Piaget, Jean. *The Psychology of the Child.* UsA: Basic Books, 1969.

Robinson, John Elder. *Be different: Adventures of a Free-Range Aspergian.* Random House of Canada, 2011.

Smith, R. S., & Sharp, J. "Fascination and Isolation: A Grounded Theory Exploration of Unusual Sensory Experiences in Adults with Asperger Syndrome." *Journal of Autism and Developmental Disorders*, 2013: 891-910.

Szatmari, P., Archer, L., Fisman, S., Streiner, D., and Wilson, F. "Asperger's Syndrrome and autism: differences in behaviour, cognition, and adaptive functioning." *Journal of American Academy of Child and Adolescent Psychiatry 34,* 1995: 1662-1671.

Tomchek, S.D., & Dunn, W. "Sensory processing in children with and without autism: A comparative study using the short sensory profile." *The American Journal of Occupational Therapy, 61(2),* 2007: 190-200.

INTERNET RESOURCES

www.davisautism.com provides information about the Davis Autism Approach Program, Davis Autism International, and referrals to Davis facilitators near you.

www.daviscanada.org provides a listing of Davis facilitators in Canada.

www.dyslexia.com is the home of Davis Dyslexia Association International.

www.noitresearch.org provides information about help for non-verbal or very young individuals with ASD.

www.oakvillesuccesscentre.ca is where you can reach Cathy Dodge Smith and Desmond Smith.

www.autismcanada.org is a Canadian national organization providing information, advocacy, and services for those living with ASD and their families, and for professionals. Links to local member associations are provided.

www.autism-society.org is a national association in the USA

which provides information, advocacy, and assistance for those living with ASD and their families, and for professionals. Links to local associations are provided.

ABOUT RONALD D. DAVIS

 Ronald D. Davis was labelled a 'Kanner's Baby' in infancy, and did not talk until the age of nine. He found his way out of the void of autism during his teen years, and with the help of speech therapy, was able to communicate verbally by the age of 17. He remained functionally illiterate until the age of 38, when he discovered the key to correcting his own dyslexia.

In 1994, he wrote and published *The Gift of Dyslexia* to answer the continuous demand from parents and educators for a book detailing the Davis Dyslexia Correction methods. Today it is published in 18 languages and is www.amazon.com's number one bestseller on the subject of dyslexia. In 2003, he wrote and published *The Gift of Learning* about his methods for correcting math (dyscalculia), handwriting (dysgraphia), and attention (ADHD) difficulties.

In February 2008, he released the Davis Autism Approach Program and began training Davis facilitators in its delivery. In October 2008, Davis Autism International was established to take his work further, and professional and parent training is now available. In 2012, Ron co-authored a book, *Autism and the Seeds of Change*, with Abigail Marshall, describing his revolutionary approach to empowering individuals with ASD to participate more fully in life.